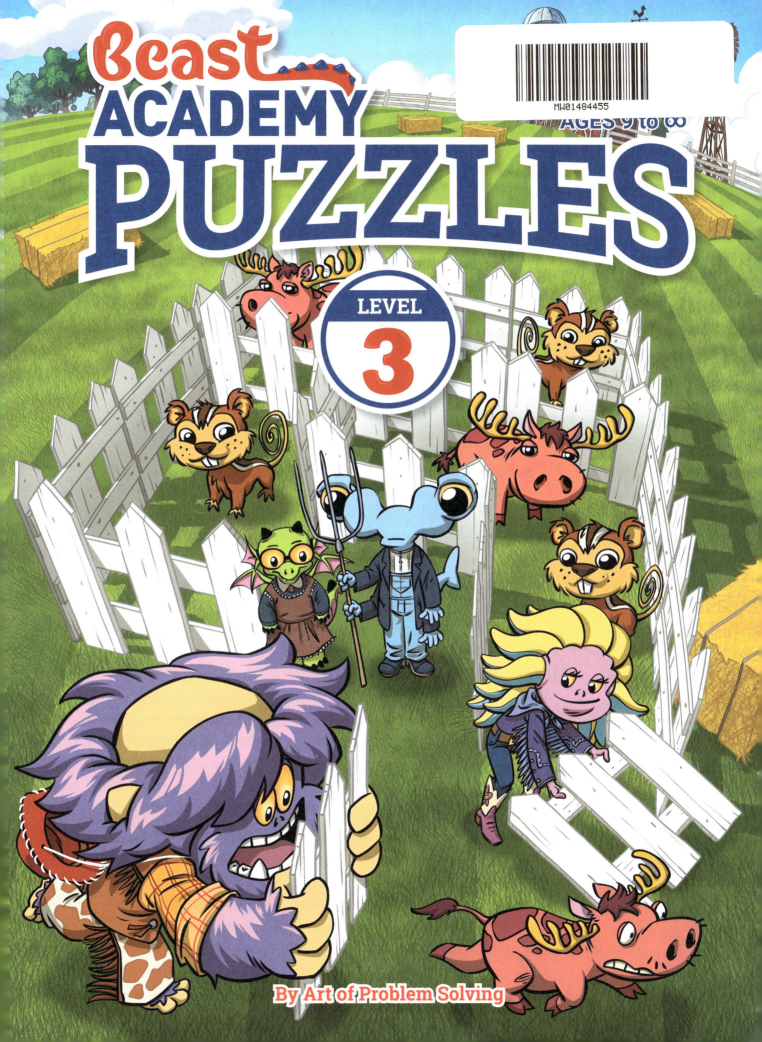

Published by:
AoPS Incorporated
10865 Rancho Bernardo Rd Ste 100
San Diego, CA 92127-2102
info@BeastAcademy.com

ISBN: 978-1-934124-58-1

Beast Academy is a registered trademark of AoPS Incorporated.

Written by Chris Page, Mark Richard, Palmer Mebane, and Jason Batterson
Book Design by Doğa Arı
Character Illustrations by Erich Owen

Visit the Beast Academy website at BeastAcademy.com.

Visit the Art of Problem Solving website at artofproblemsolving.com.

Printed in the United States of America.
First Printing 2020.

CONTENTS

ABOUT THIS BOOK

Beast Academy Puzzles 3 contains nearly 500 puzzles in 12 different styles. Every puzzle style is aligned with the broader Beast Academy level 3 math curriculum. Whether used on their own or as part of the complete Beast Academy curriculum, these puzzles will delight and entertain puzzle solvers of all ages.

The puzzles in this book cover a broad range of topics including angle classification, skip-counting, multiplication, division, perimeter, area, and the basics of fractions and variables as taught in the Beast Academy level 3 series. The difficulty ranges from straightforward puzzles meant to give a feel for how each puzzle works to diabolical stumpers written by world puzzle champion Palmer Mebane.

WHY PUZZLES?

Entertainment

Puzzles intrigue us and capture our attention in ways that many other problems don't. What makes puzzles so captivating?

- **Breakthroughs.** The "Aha!" moments of ingenuity and insight that come when solving a well-written puzzle are energizing.

- **Satisfaction.** Not every puzzle has an "Aha!" moment of inspiration. Many involve a series of steps that are satisfying and encouraging in their own way.

- **Accomplishment.** Solving a puzzle that is just at the edge of your ability level gives a wonderful sense of achievement.

- **Gratification.** Unlike many other problems you face, it's often immediately obvious when you've solved a puzzle correctly.

Enrichment

Solving puzzles makes us smarter. What do we learn?

- **Problem Solving.** The skills we learn by solving puzzles— observing, testing, fiddling, and making connections—help us become better, more resilient problem solvers in other areas.

- **Math Skills.** Every puzzle in this book was written to reinforce specific math skills. Puzzles take the monotony out of skill drill and make practice fun.

- **Spatial Reasoning.** Many puzzles require elements of path tracing or grouping that help us build spatial awareness.

- **Pattern Recognition.** Solving puzzles helps us recognize patterns and encourages us to search for new ones.

Angle Mazes

Connect the Critters

Skip-Counting Paths

Fence 'Em In

Fillominoes

Times Out

Product Squares

Arranging Squares

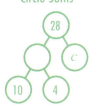

Circle Sums

Fraction Link

Abstract Art

Shikaku

USING THIS BOOK

This book is divided by puzzle type into 12 sections, followed by HINTS beginning on page 163 and SOLUTIONS beginning on page 185.

Each section includes instructions, a solved example, and difficulty ratings. The ratings at the edge of the page refer to the difficulty of the hardest problem on the page and are highly subjective.

At the end of each puzzle set is a STRATEGIES section. We highly recommend reading the strategies section even if you've already solved all of the puzzles. There may be an approach you haven't considered.

Supplementing the BA Curriculum

If you are using this book to supplement the Beast Academy math curriculum, below is a list of the different puzzle types, the chapters they supplement in BA level 3, and what math skills they reinforce.

Angle Mazes	Chapter 1	Identifying angle types. Adapted from Practice book 3A.
Connect the Critters	Chapter 1	Spatial reasoning. Find more like this in BA Online.
Skip-Counting Paths	Chapter 2	Skip-counting. Adapted from Practice book 5C.
Fence 'Em In	Chapter 3	Perimeter and area. Find more like this in BA Online.
Fillominoes	Chapter 3	Area and spatial reasoning. Find more like this in BA Online.
Times Out	Chapter 4	Multiplication and division. Adapted from Practice book 4B.
Product Squares	Chapter 4	Multiplication and division. New puzzle!
Arranging Squares	Chapter 5	Recognizing perfect squares. Find more in Practice book 3B.
Circle Sums	Chapter 7	Variables and expressions. Find more in Practice book 3C.
Fraction Link	Chapter 10	Fraction conversions. Find more in Practice book 3D.
Abstract Art	Chapter 10	Fractions. Find more like this in BA Online.
Shikaku	Chapter 12	Rectangle area. Find more like this in BA Online.

ANGLE MAZES
DIFFICULTY LEVEL:
★—★★★★★

In an **Angle Maze**, the goal is to draw a path through the maze that uses each given angle type in order.

The path begins at the start arrow, makes turns that match the listed angles in order, and leaves at the exit arrow.

The path may not use a line segment twice.

The path may pass straight through any dot, and may visit the same dot more than once.

Trace a path that uses the given angle types.

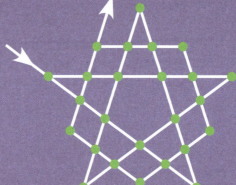

1. Obtuse
2. Obtuse
3. Acute
4. Obtuse

Beginning at the start arrow, the path takes an obtuse turn at the dot labeled 1, an obtuse turn at 2, an acute turn at 3, and an obtuse turn at 4, then finishes at the exit arrow.

This is the only possible path between these arrows with the angles given.

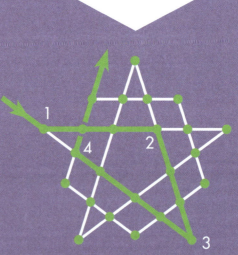

1. Obtuse
2. Obtuse
3. Acute
4. Obtuse

1.

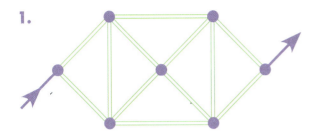

1. Acute
2. Right
3. Obtuse

2.

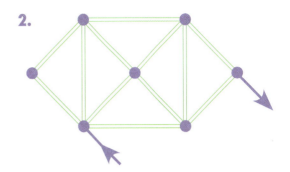

1. Acute
2. Acute
3. Acute
4. Obtuse

3.

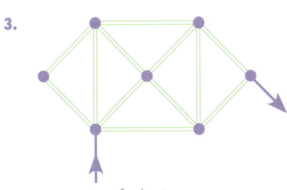

1. Acute
2. Right
3. Obtuse
4. Right
5. Acute

4.

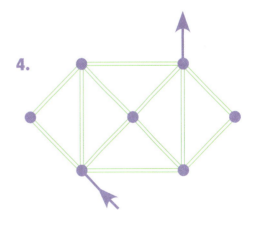

1. Right
2. Right
3. Right
4. Right
5. Right
6. Acute

5.

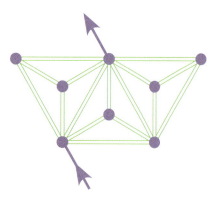

1. Acute
2. Acute
3. Acute

6.

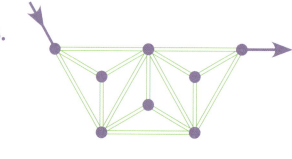

1. Right
2. Obtuse
3. Right

7.

1. Acute
2. Obtuse
3. Right
4. Acute

8.

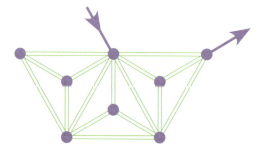

1. Right
2. Obtuse
3. Right
4. Right
5. Obtuse

9.

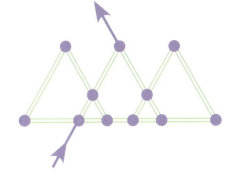

1. Acute
2. Obtuse
3. Acute

10.

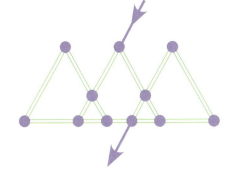

1. Acute
2. Acute
3. Acute
4. Acute

11.

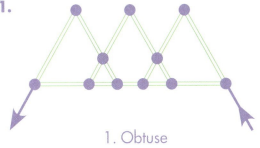

1. Obtuse
2. Acute
3. Obtuse
4. Acute

12.

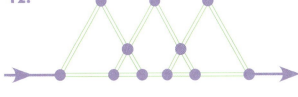

1. Acute
2. Obtuse
3. Acute
4. Obtuse
5. Acute

13.

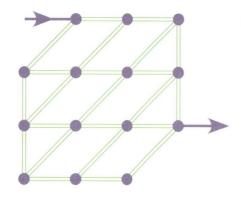

1. Right
2. Obtuse
3. Acute

⊕ 14.

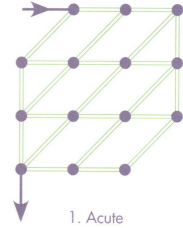

1. Acute
2. Obtuse
3. Acute
4. Acute
5. Right

⊕ 15.

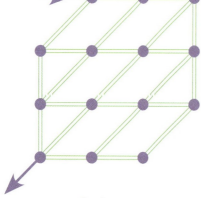

1. Acute
2. Obtuse
3. Obtuse
4. Obtuse
5. Obtuse

⊕ 16.

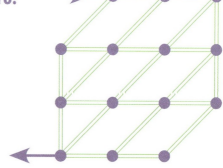

1. Acute
2. Obtuse
3. Obtuse
4. Acute
5. Obtuse
6. Obtuse
7. Acute
8. Obtuse

H 17.

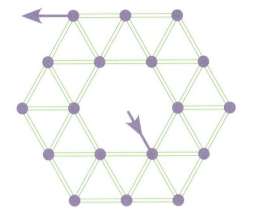

1. Acute
2. Acute
3. Acute

H 18.

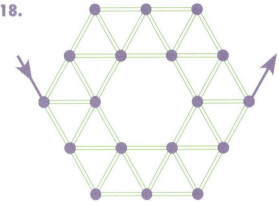

1. Acute
2. Acute
3. Acute

H 19.

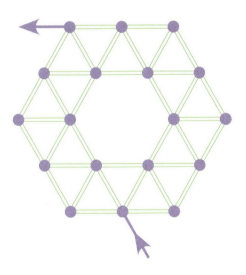

1. Acute
2. Obtuse
3. Acute
4. Acute

H 20.

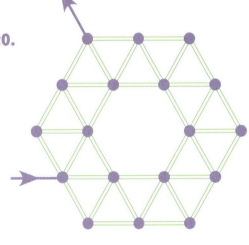

1. Acute
2. Obtuse
3. Acute
4. Obtuse
5. Obtuse
6. Obtuse
7. Acute

H **21.**

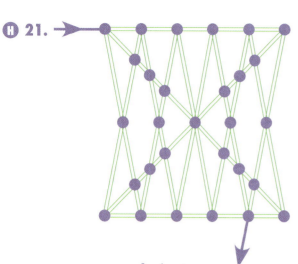

1. Acute
2. Right
3. Obtuse

H **22.**

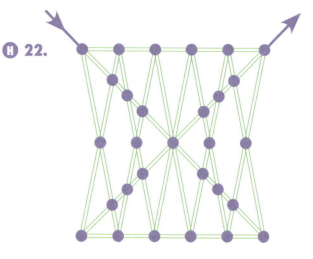

1. Right
2. Obtuse
3. Acute
4. Acute
5. Right

H **23.**

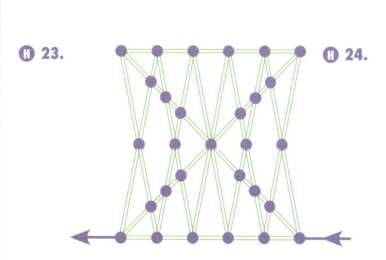

1. Acute
2. Acute
3. Right
4. Obtuse
5. Obtuse

H **24.**

1. Obtuse
2. Acute
3. Right
4. Obtuse
5. Acute

H 25.

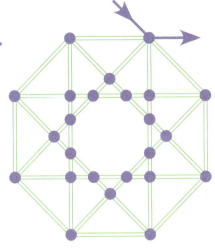

1. Acute
2. Acute
3. Acute
4. Acute
5. Acute

H 26.

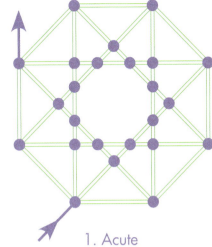

1. Acute
2. Obtuse
3. Acute
4. Obtuse
5. Acute

H 27.

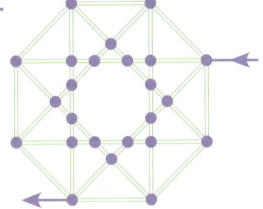

1. Right
2. Acute
3. Acute
4. Obtuse
5. Obtuse
6. Right

H 28.

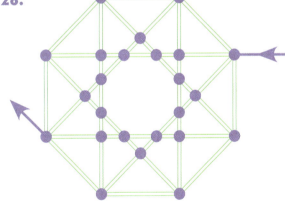

1. Right
2. Right
3. Right
4. Right
5. Right
6. Obtuse
7. Obtuse
8. Obtuse

ANGLE MAZES
STRATEGIES

1. Number known points.

Labeling known turns of the maze helps us keep track of the current path.

2. Work backwards.

Sometimes there are fewer choices if we start at the end and work backwards.

How can we solve this maze while working backwards?

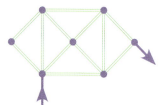

1. Acute
2. Right
3. Obtuse
4. Right
5. Acute

Step 5 is an acute angle. There is only one acute angle at the end of our path.

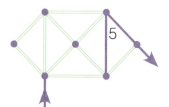

1. Acute
2. Right
3. Obtuse
4. Right
5. Acute

Step 4 is a right angle. There is only one right angle that lets us continue the path.

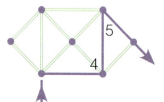

1. Acute
2. Right
3. Obtuse
4. Right
5. Acute

We can continue working backwards to solve the puzzle.

(Also, try alternating between working backwards and working forwards.)

3. Stay organized.

When we have several possible paths, we can look at every possibility and stay organized so that we can eliminate paths that don't work.

Where are the first turns in the angle maze below?

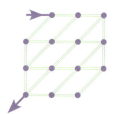

1. Acute
2. Obtuse
3. Obtuse
4. Obtuse
5. Obtuse

There are three possible choices for step 1:

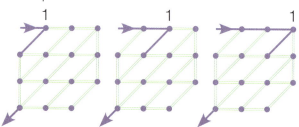

If we turn at the first dot in step 1, there is only one choice for step 2. Then, there is only one more obtuse angle the path can follow. This path only uses three angles, so we eliminate it.

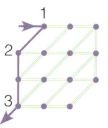

If we turn at the second dot in step 1, there are two choices for step 2.

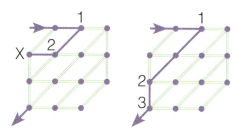

On the left, there are no choices for a second obtuse angle. On the right, the only choice for a second obtuse angle creates a path with only three angles. So, we eliminate these choices.

This leaves the third choice for step 1. For this case, there are two choices for step 2:

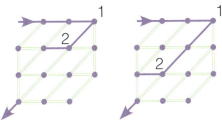

We continue this way, looking at all possibilities, until the entire path is complete.

4. Look for unusual angles or groups of angles.

Sometimes an angle or group of angles only appears in a few places in the grid.

Which right angles are in the maze below?

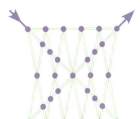

1. Right
2. Obtuse
3. Acute
4. Acute
5. Right

The only right angles in the maze are where the two diagonal lines cross in the center. We label the first and fifth angles of the path.

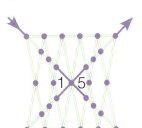

1. Right
2. Obtuse
3. Acute
4. Acute
5. Right

5. Draw outside of the maze.

Try sketching on paper what the path could look like without worrying about specific dots.

What could the path look like?

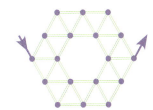

1. Acute
2. Acute
3. Acute

The path begins going down and to the right, and ends going up and to the right.

There are several ways we can connect these arrows using three acute angles.

We can rule out paths that can't fit, like the path on the left. Then, we look for ways to fit the paths we've drawn on the maze.

(This strategy works best when the lines of the maze are only drawn in a few different directions.)

6. Explore options.

Sometimes it's easy to get stuck trying the same path time after time after time.

Explore parts of the maze you have not looked at, or take time away to get fresh insights.

CONNECT THE CRITTERS

DIFFICULTY LEVEL:

In a **Connect the Critters** puzzle, the goal is to connect all the critters using the set of polyominoes (shapes made of connected squares) given at the top of the page.

The polyominoes and the critters must form a single closed shape.

Pieces that only touch at the corners do not count as connected.

Polyominoes can only cover white squares. They cannot cover critters, solid squares, other polyominoes, or regions outside the grid.

Cut out the shapes on the next page to help you solve these puzzles.

Use the pieces below to connect the Chipmonkeys to each other.

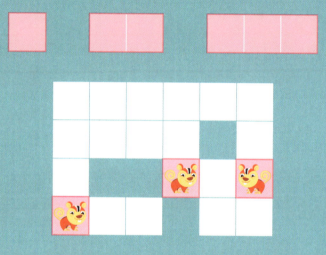

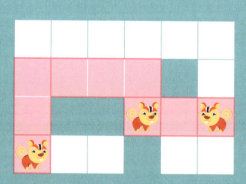

Print more polyominoes at BeastAcademy.com/Resources

Cut out the polyominoes below to help you solve the puzzles that follow.

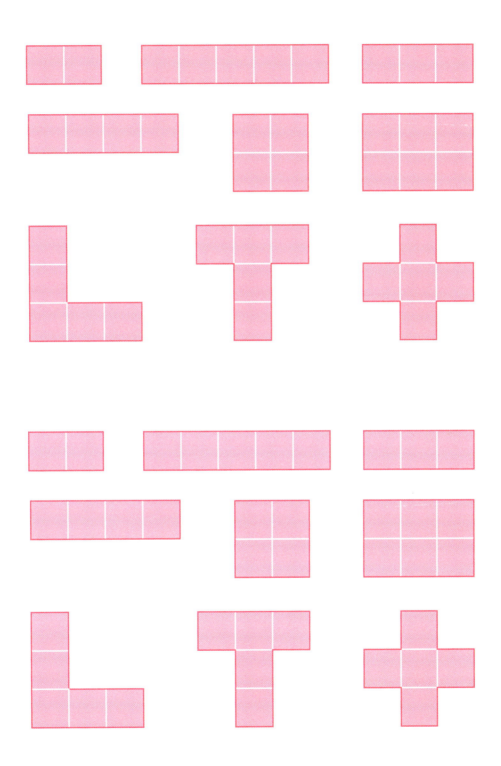

CONNECT THE CRITTERS

Print more copies of these polyominoes at BeastAcademy.com/Resources

Cut out the polyominoes on the back of this page to help you solve the puzzles that follow.

Use the pieces below to connect the Porcupumas in the puzzles on this page.

1.

2.

3.

4.

5.

6.

Use the pieces below to connect the Tortusks in the puzzles on this page.

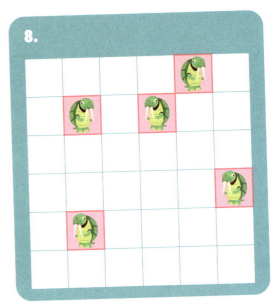

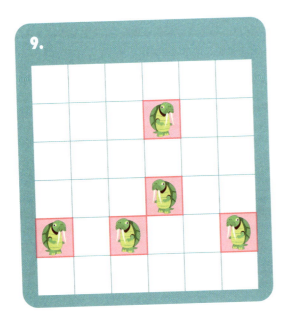

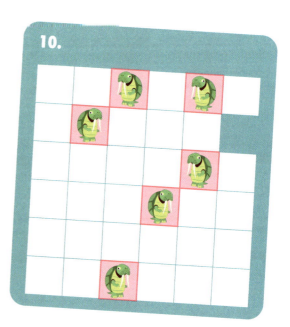

Use the pieces below to connect the Pelicamels in the puzzles on this page.

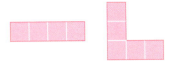

★ ★ ☆ ☆ ☆

11.

12.

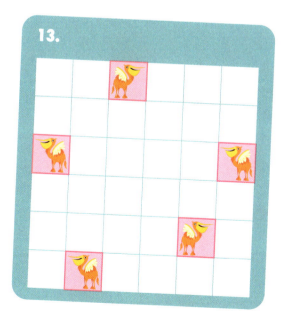

13.

14.

Use the pieces below to connect the Hippopotamoose in the puzzles on this page.

15.

16.

17.

18.

Use the pieces below to connect the Alligophers in the puzzles on this page.

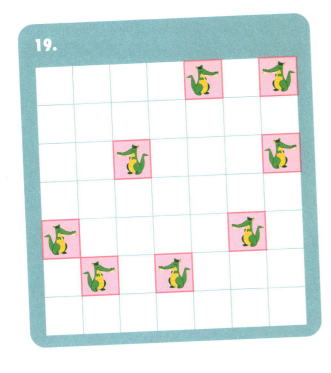

19.

20.

21.

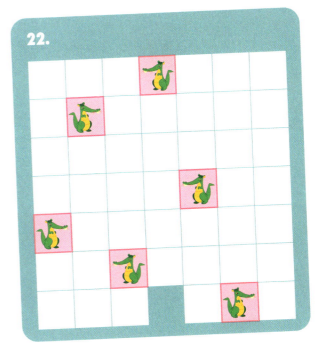

22.

Use the pieces below to connect the Jackalopes in the puzzles on this page.

23.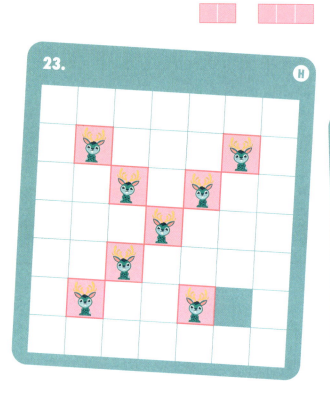

24.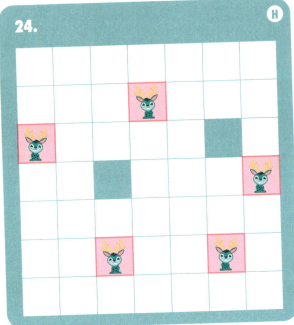

25.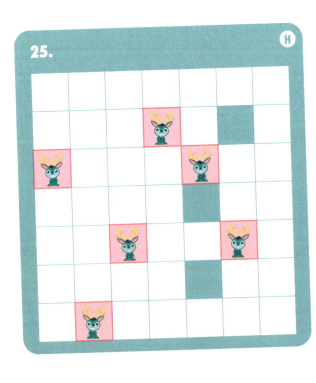

26.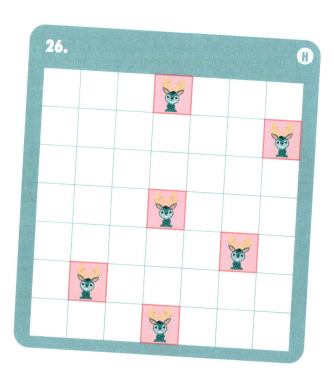

Use the pieces below to connect the Orangutoads in the puzzles on this page.

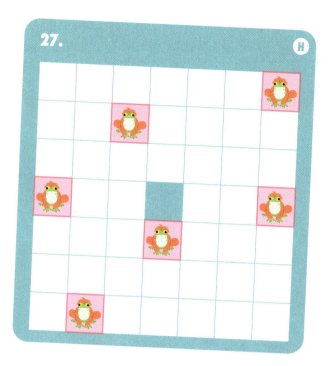

27.

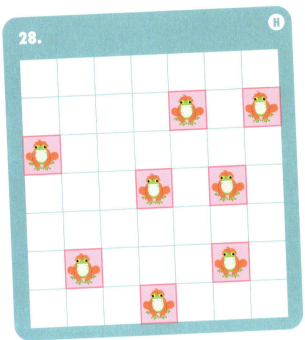

28.

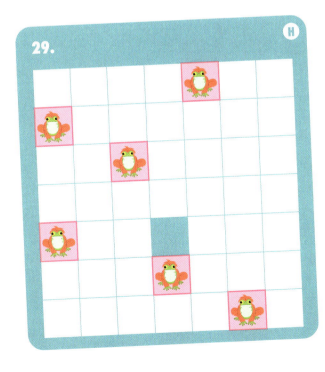

29.

30.

Hints on pages 165-166

☆ ★ ★ ★ ★

Use the pieces below to connect the Buffalobsters in the puzzles on this page.

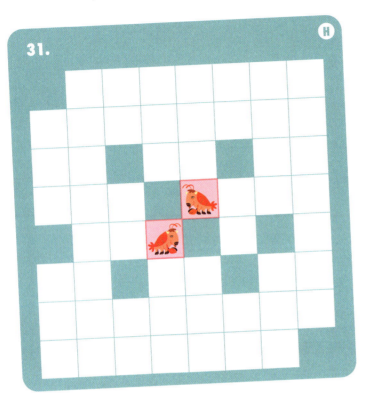

31.

32.

Hints on pages 165-166 and Beast Academy Puzzles 3

Hints on pages 165-166   Beast Academy Puzzles 3

Use the pieces below to connect the Rhincocerabbits in the puzzles on this page.

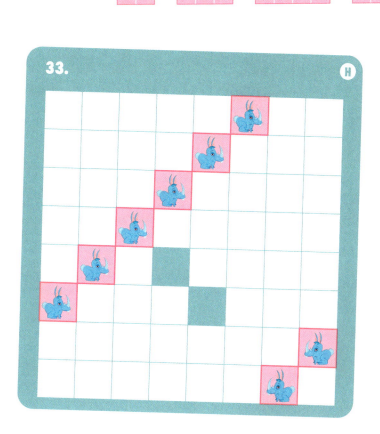

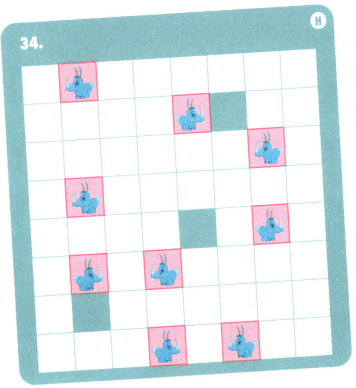

H Hints on pages 165-166

CONNECT THE CRITTERS
STRATEGIES

1. Cut out the pieces.

It's much easier to keep track of physical pieces than to try and solve these mentally.

2. Try something!

Experiment! Play with the pieces. Move them. Turn them around.

When we're stuck, we try some of the strategies below.

3. Try having each piece connect as many critters as possible.

In almost every puzzle, there are more critters than pieces, so some pieces must touch several critters.

Where can we place the L-shaped piece so it touches 3 critters?

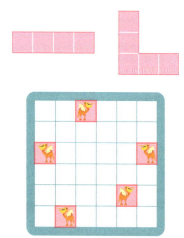

There are two ways we can use the L-piece to connect three critters. We can then try the remaining piece in both these options.

(If neither works, try placing the L-piece to connect two critters.)

4. Search every placement.

Some pieces can only be placed in a few locations.

Where can we place the plus-shaped piece?

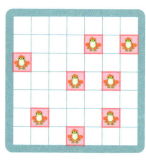

There are six locations where we can place the plus-shaped piece:

We first try the locations where the plus-shaped piece is touching two or three critters.

(We can even repeat this strategy on each of these six choices with another piece, but we need to keep our work organized.)

5. Find a critter that can only be reached by some of the pieces.

Which critter can only be reached by one piece?

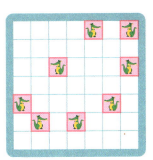

The top-right square can only be reached by the 1-by-2 rectangle. So, we must place this rectangle in one of these two places:

6. Take a break.

Sometimes it's easy to get stuck placing the piece in the same location every time. Try a mental reset. Work with a different piece, turn the book upside down, or just take a rest and try the puzzle some other time.

SKIP-COUNTING PATHS

DIFFICULTY LEVEL:

In a **Skip-Counting Paths** puzzle, the goal is to draw one or more paths that connect **at least three numbers** in order to form a skip-counting pattern using the following rules:

- Each skip-counting pattern uses multiples of the number we're skip-counting by. For example, we can use 25, 30, 35, 40, which are all multiples of 5, but not 26, 31, 36, 41.

- Every number must be part of exactly one path.

- Paths can only travel up, down, left, or right (not diagonally).

- No two paths can cross the same square.

- If solved correctly, the paths will use every square in the grid.

Since 15 is the smallest number in the grid, it must be one end of a path. Starting from 15, we can skip-count by 3's or by 5's:

15, 18, 20, 21, 24, 25

15, 18, 20, 21, 24, 25

Only 15-20-25 leaves numbers that also form a skip-counting pattern: 18-21-24. So, we connect the numbers in these skip-counting patterns in order, as shown to the right.

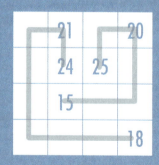

★ ☆ ☆ ☆ ☆

1.

4	16		8
		12	

2.

30			
24			
		18	
21		27	

3.

	24	50	
		25	75
		16	8

4.

	77		
	63		
		70	
91		84	

5.

16	20		6
	3	12	
			9

6.

6			27
	12	30	
	21		
	18		24

7.

22	20	12	
	16		14
		24	18

8.

63	50		
		45	
54		36	
60	55		

9.

88			11
		22	55
		33	66
77			44

10.

	32		30	
	48			
40		24		
35				25

11.

6		15		
		3		
	12			10
		9		
20				5

12.

48				16
	12	6	4	
		32	8	
	40	2		

13.

	49			
			60	42
		35	45	
56				30

14.

	45			
	60	18	9	
			54	
36	42		48	
	27			

15.

36				30
		24		
	35	20		
		40		
32		28		25

Beast Academy Puzzles 3

H 16.

			12	24
	21	18		
		20		
			15	
16				

H 17.

18				12
		3		
		15		
			21	9
6				

H 18.

				40
25		20		60
		80	30	
	35			

H 19.

8		30		
	10		24	
	14			28
12		16	32	26

H 20.

30			24	14
	25			21
	35	27		
20			15	28

H 21.

65				60
	80	45		40
75		70	30	
15				20

H Hints on page 167

H 22.

		30	45		
		15	9		
	6	3	8	20	
	12			16	

H 23.

27					14
	44			30	
		33	55		
		24	42		
	35			66	
28					21

H 24.

62			63		
		42	36		84
	93				
	21	31	12	48	24

H 25.

		35	7		18
	24		30	40	48	14
45	36		42		21

H 26.

77	66	63	48	42	26
88	81	56	49	36	28
99	90	45	32	40	30
80	70	50	24	18	21
96	60	55	39	15	4
84	72	65	52	12	8

H 27.

55			96		84
80			66		
		72	60		
		90		77	
70					

H Hints on page 167

Beast Academy Puzzles 3

H 28.

			56	
	40			
36			44	45
	54			52
		48		

H 29.

21			15	14
30		20		
			28	
	35			
		25		

H 30.

8	12				14
		22			20
			16		
24				10	
18					

H 31.

			9		72
	81				
	36				
			45		
	18			27	
54					63

H 32.

40		20		22	
				12	
48		8	24	32	
					4
18					16

H 33.

32	24				16
		64		20	
				40	
	48				
	80		36		
96				60	12

H Hints on page 167

☆
★
★
★
★

H 34.

48					45	
30	55	60	15	24	65	40
	50			70		
		32				

H 35.

					48
	63	36			
		81			
	24			30	
72			42		
54					60

H 36.

27				35
		42		39
		28		
	36		33	
	24			21
30				

H 37.

			54		48
		60		50	
	55		30		
65					56
	80			42	
	70		36		
72		64			

H Hints on page 167

38.

							60
	42				55		
44				56			
				50			
	66						
				70	63		
						65	
49		48				46	

39.

Hints on page 167

SKIP-COUNTING PATHS
STRATEGIES

1. Start with the smallest or largest number.

The smallest number must be the first number in a skip-counting pattern that is at least 3 numbers long.

Which numbers must be connected to the smallest number in the puzzle below?

48				16
	12	6	4	
		32	8	
	40	2		

One pattern starts with 2. We can only skip-count by 2's: 2-4-6. While 8 may be part of this pattern, it may be needed for a different pattern, so we do not yet include it.

So, we must connect 2-4-6.

2. Find numbers that can only be used in a few skip-counting patterns.

What skip-counting pattern is 31 part of?

62			63		
		42	36		84
	93				
	21	31	12	48	24

Since there is no number you can use to skip-count to 31, it must be the start of a skip-counting pattern. Skip-counting by 31's gives 31-62-93.

3. Look for numbers with limited path options on the grid.

Some numbers have only a few possible connections.

What path includes the 14?

30			24	14
	25			21
	35	27		
20		15	28	

The 14 in the top-right corner can only be connected to the 21 or the 24. We cannot make a skip-counting pattern using 14 and 24. So, we make a skip-counting by 7's pattern using 14-21-28.

We connect these numbers on the grid.

30			24	14
	25			21
	35	27		
20		15	28	

4. List all the numbers in order.

Listing all of the numbers in the grid in order makes it easier to find the skip-counting patterns.

Which two skip-counting patterns must be used to complete the puzzle below?

The numbers in the grid are 36, 40, 44, 45, 48, 52, 54, and 56. We start with the smallest number, 36.

Skip-counting from 36 by 4's gives a skip-counting pattern of 36-40-44. However, this makes it impossible to use 45 in a skip-counting pattern.

36, 40, 44, 45, 48, 52, 54, 56

Skip-counting from 36 by 9's gives a skip-counting pattern of 36-45-54. Then, the remaining five numbers form a second skip-counting pattern.

36, 40, 44, 45, 48, 52, 54, 56

There is no other skip-counting pattern we can create starting with 36. So, the two skip-counting patterns are 36-45-54 and 40-44-48-52-56.

(Be sure to count the number of numbers in the grid, and make sure it matches the length of the list!)

5. Connect the known pieces.

Sometimes a number can be part of more than one skip-counting pattern. In this case, we connect the parts we are sure of, then sort the remaining numbers.

What path includes the 11? The 88?

The numbers in the grid are 11, 22, 33, 44, 55, 66, 77, and 88.

The smallest number, 11, can only be the first number in a skip-counting pattern by 11's. There is only one way to connect 11, 22, and 33.

This path may continue to 44, or it can stop at 33 since it is already three numbers long. Since we're not sure, we can work in another part of the grid and come back later.

The largest number, 88, is the end of another skip-counting pattern. Now, we can only connect 88 to 77. We are skip-counting by 11's, so we then connect 77 to 66.

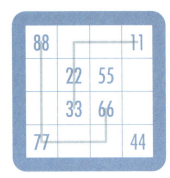

(Sometimes it even helps to draw the beginning or end of a path between two numbers.)

6. Don't draw paths that block other paths.

Make sure a path doesn't block other paths, numbers, or regions.

How can we connect 3 to 6?

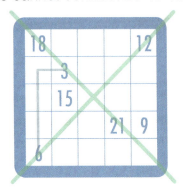

Starting with 3, we have a path that includes 3-6-9. Starting with 21 and counting down, we have a path that includes 21-18-15.

If we connect 3 to 6 as shown below, then we cannot connect 21-18-15.

So, we connect 3 to 6 as shown below, making sure we can still connect 6 to 9.

7. Connect numbers along the edges of the grid.

Connecting numbers along the edge of the grid doesn't block other paths, and lets us use all of the squares on the grid.

What path begins with the 8 below?

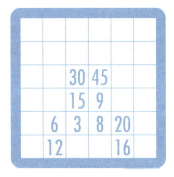

The 8 can only be part of the skip-counting pattern 8-12-16. There is only one way to connect 8 to 12.

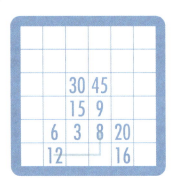

Then, we connect 12 to 16 with a path along the edge of the grid as shown.

After connecting 12 to 16, the "edges" of the grid are now inside the new path.

(Now, how can we connect 3-6-9 around the new "edges" of the grid?)

8. Guess!

When stuck, try something and see what happens. Keep track of which guesses don't work.

Don't worry about drawing something wrong. That's what erasers are for!

FENCE 'EM IN
DIFFICULTY LEVEL:
★—★★★★★

In a **Fence 'Em In** puzzle, we draw pens that have the same area and perimeter to separate critters.

Each pen should contain exactly one of each type of critter.

Each pen must have the given area and perimeter.

Area: 3
Perimeter: 8

Since critters of the same type can't be inside the same pen, we draw a fence between the two chipmonkeys in the left corner.

The chipmonkey on the bottom-left must share a pen with the hippopotamoose to its right. There is only one way to enclose a pen for these two critters with area 3 and perimeter 8.

Then, we close the two other pens as shown to complete the puzzle.

1. Area: 3
Perimeter: 8

2. Area: 5
Perimeter: 12

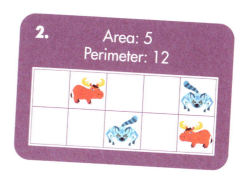

3. Area: 5
Perimeter: 10

4. Area: 4
Perimeter: 10

5. Area: 4
Perimeter: 8

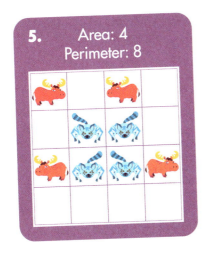

6. Area: 4
Perimeter: 10

7. Area: 4
Perimeter: 10 Ⓗ

8. Area: 5
Perimeter: 12 Ⓗ

9. Area: 4
Perimeter: 10 Ⓗ

10. Area: 3
Perimeter: 8 Ⓗ

11. Area: 4
Perimeter: 10 Ⓗ

12. Area: 6
Perimeter: 12 Ⓗ

13. Area: 3
Perimeter: 8

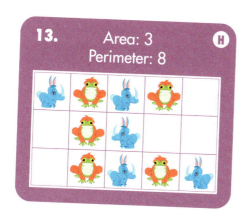

14. Area: 4
Perimeter: 10

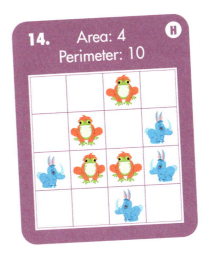

15. Area: 5
Perimeter: 12

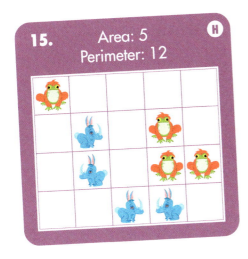

16. Area: 5
Perimeter: 12

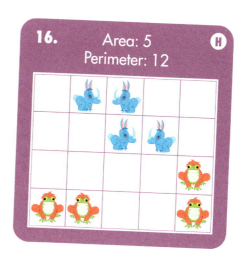

17. Area: 5
Perimeter: 10

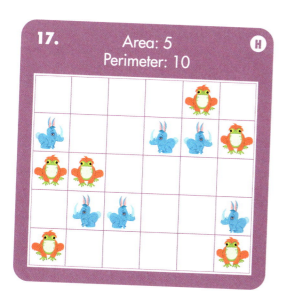

18. Area: 6
Perimeter: 10

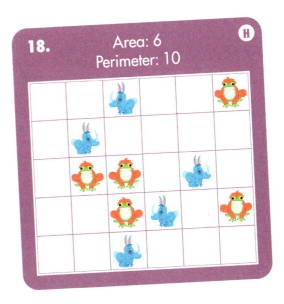

H Hints on pages 168-169

19. Area: 5
Perimeter: 12 Ⓗ

20. Area: 5
Perimeter: 10 Ⓗ

21. Area: 5
Perimeter: 12 Ⓗ

22. Area: 7
Perimeter: 16 Ⓗ

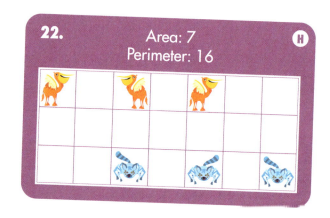

23. Area: 8
Perimeter: 18 Ⓗ

24. Area: 5
Perimeter: 12 Ⓗ

25. Area: 8
Perimeter: 12

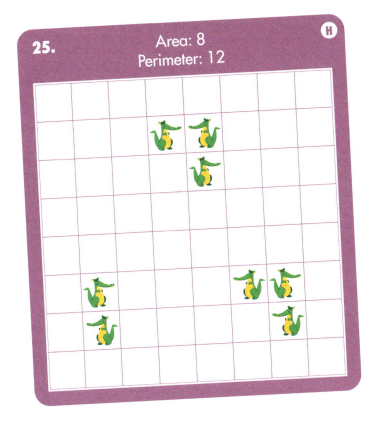

26. Area: 6
Perimeter: 14

27. Area: 6
Perimeter: 12

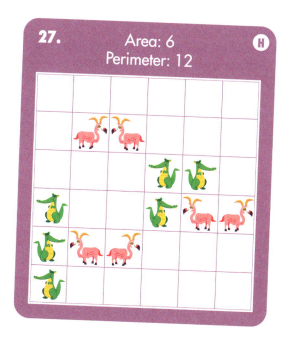

28. Area: 4
Perimeter: 10

Hints on pages 168-169

29. Area: 10
Perimeter: 14

30. Area: 7
Perimeter: 14

31. Area: 8
Perimeter: 14

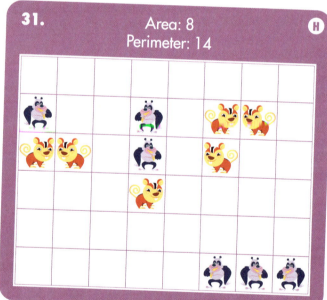

32. Area: 6
Perimeter: 12

33. Area: 6
Perimeter: 14 Ⓗ

34. Area: 7
Perimeter: 12 Ⓗ

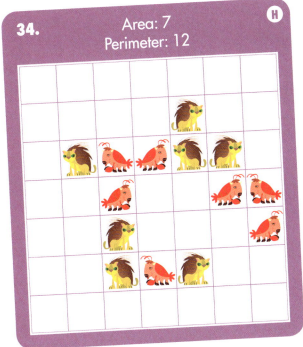

35. Area: 8
Perimeter: 16 Ⓗ

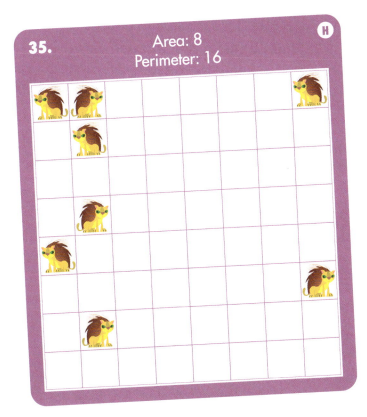

36. Area: 9
Perimeter: 20 Ⓗ

FENCE 'EM IN
STRATEGIES

1. Draw fences between critters of the same type.

Two critters of the same type can't be in the same pen. So, we can draw fences between them.

Which fences can we immediately place?

We draw fences between all touching octopugs, and between all touching chimpandas.

2. Find an easy pen to draw first.

Drawing one pen will limit where the other pens can go.

What pen is the highlighted octopug part of?

There is only one chimpanda that can be part of the same pen as the octopug.

Then, there is only one jackalope we can include in this pen and still have area 4. This pen also has perimeter 10, so we draw it.

(Then, what pen is the bottom-left jackalope part of?)

3. Find possible pen shapes using rectangles.

Sketch all of the rectangles that have the given perimeter, then see how they can be modified to give the correct area.

What shapes have a perimeter 14 and area 10?

There are three different rectangles we can make with perimeter 14:

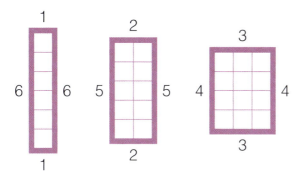

The 1×6 rectangle has area 6, so we can't use it.

The 2×5 rectangle has area 10, so we can use it as a pen.

The 3×4 rectangle has perimeter 14, but area 12. So, we can't make pens that are 3-by-4 rectangles. But, we can modify this shape to reduce its area without changing its perimeter.

For example, we can remove the corner squares of the rectangle to create a shape with area 10 and perimeter 14.

Area: 12   Area: 10
Perimeter: 14   Perimeter: 14

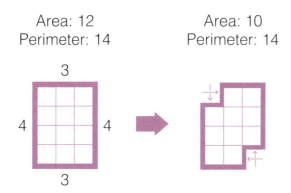

Below are more shapes with area 10 and perimeter 14 that can be created by removing squares from the corners.

Careful! This only works for removing squares that have two sides on the perimeter. The shape below has area 10, but perimeter 18, not 14.

4. Match critters that must be connected.

Which octopugs are connected to which chimpandas?

Each octopug in the left column can only be connected to one chimpanda.

Then there is only one way to connect each of the remaining octopugs to a chimpanda.

Now, how can you draw the pens?

5. Don't isolate empty squares or critters.

How can we connect the highlighted pelicamel to a tarantulemur?

There are two possible tarantulemurs that could be part of a pen with area 5 that contains the highlighted pelicamel.

If we connect the highlighted pelicamel to the tarantulemur in the third row, then there is no way to connect the tarantulemur in the fourth row to a pelicamel.

So, we connect the highlighted pelicamel to the tarantulemur in the fourth row.

Then, there is only one way to connect these two critters in a pen of area 5 without leaving any isolated squares.

6. Identify "skinny" pens.

How can we make pens with area 8 that have the largest possible perimeter, 18?

We can build pen shapes with area 8 by attaching one square at a time.

One square has perimeter 4.

Perimeter: 4

When we attach a square to one of its sides, we get a shape with a perimeter of 6.

Perimeter: 6

Each time we attach a new square to one of the existing squares, we increase the shape's perimeter by 2. (The new square covers one side of an existing square, but adds three new sides to the shape's perimeter.)

Perimeter:

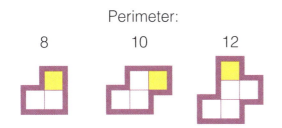

But, if we add a square that connects to *two* of the existing squares, we don't increase the perimeter of the shape. (The shape covers two sides of squares, and adds two new sides to the shape's perimeter.)

Perimeter:

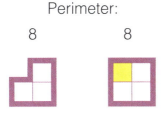

So, to make the perimeter as large as possible, we attach squares one at a time so that they only touch one other square.

This results in shapes that are all "skinny" like the ones below. They all have area 8 and perimeter 18.

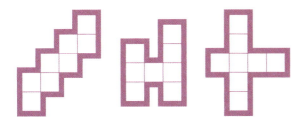

A "skinny" shape can never contain a 2-by-2 square. The shapes below are not skinny.

(See Strategy #8 for more.)

7. **Connect squares that must be part of the same pen.**

Sometimes squares can only be part of one pen.

Which squares are part of the pens for the flamingoats in the bottom row?

We first use strategy 1 to draw fences between pens of the same type of critter.

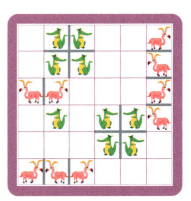

The pens containing the two flamingoats in the bottom left must include the squares directly above them.

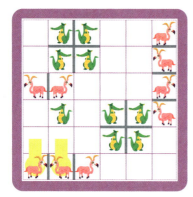

Then, the bottom-left pen can only be extended one way and still include an alligopher.

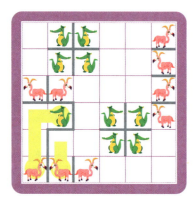

Then, there is only one way we can complete the partially drawn pen.

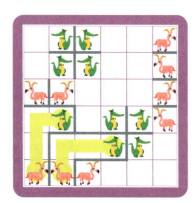

Finally, there is only one pen we can complete with the remaining flamingoat in the bottom row.

8. Modify pens without changing their area and perimeter.

Once we find a pen shape that has the correct area and perimeter, it's easier to find other pen shapes that work, too.

The shape below has area 6 and perimeter 12.

The shapes below also have area 6. Which have the same perimeter as the shape above?

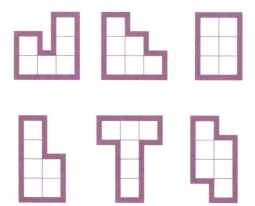

Notice that if we remove a square that touches just one other square, we can attach it to one side of a new square without changing the area or perimeter of the shape.

So, these three shapes all have the same perimeter as the original shape.

(Notice that all of these shapes have a single 2-by-2 region with two squares attached to it. These are not "skinny" pens, but they are easy to spot. In fact, any pen with area 6 and perimeter 12 will have one 2-by-2 region.)

FILLOMINOES
DIFFICULTY LEVEL:

In a **Fillomino** puzzle, the goal is to fill squares in a grid to create polyominoes (shapes made of connected squares) with the given areas.

Every square in the grid must be filled with a number that gives the area of the polyomino it is a part of.

In each puzzle, there must be exactly one polyomino of each of the given areas.

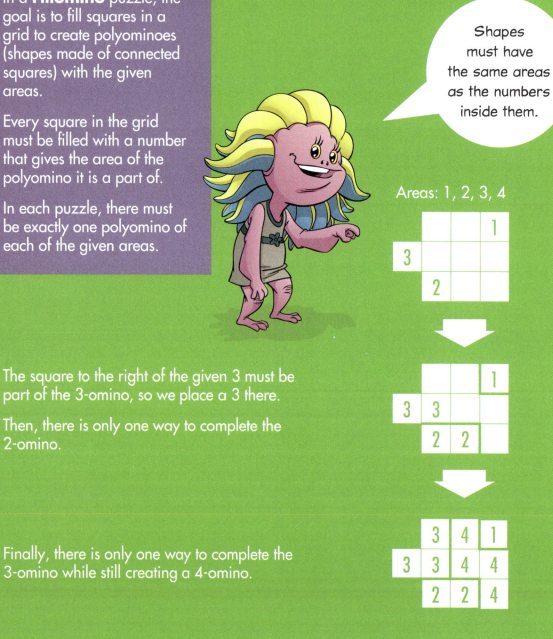

Shapes must have the same areas as the numbers inside them.

The square to the right of the given 3 must be part of the 3-omino, so we place a 3 there.

Then, there is only one way to complete the 2-omino.

Finally, there is only one way to complete the 3-omino while still creating a 4-omino.

Instead of writing a number in every square, we could also draw lines connecting all the squares of each polyomino.

1. Areas: 2, 3, 4

2. Areas: 1, 3, 5

1	3	
	5	

3. Areas: 3, 4, 5

4. Areas: 1, 2, 3, 6

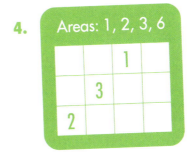

5. Areas: 1, 2, 4, 5

2		5
	1	4

6. Areas: 2, 4, 6

	4	
	2	4
	6	

7. Areas: 1, 2, 3, 4

	1	
3		4
	2	

8. Areas: 1, 2, 3, 4

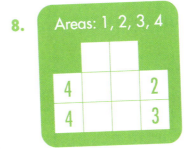

9. Areas: 1, 2, 4, 5

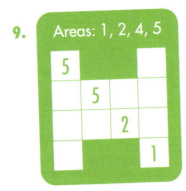

10. Areas: 1, 2, 3, 4

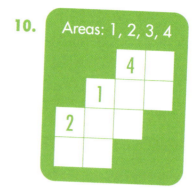

11. Areas: 1, 4, 5, 6

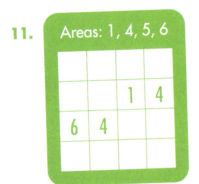

12. Areas: 4, 5, 7

13. Areas: 1, 2, 3, 4, 5, 6

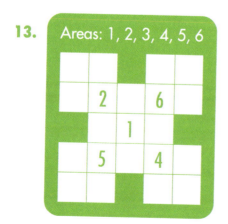

14. Areas: 2, 3, 4, 7

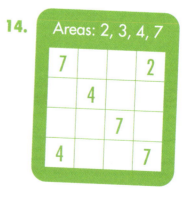

15. 1, 2, 3, 4, 6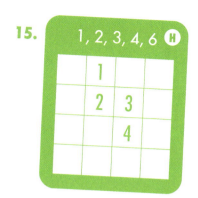

16. Areas: 2, 3, 4, 5, 6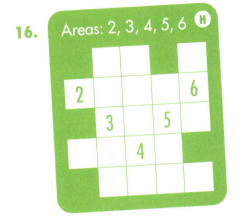

17. Areas: 2, 3, 5, 6, 7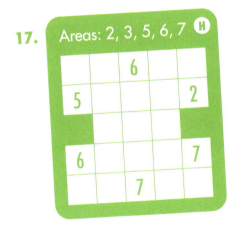

18. Areas: 5, 6, 7

19. Areas: 1, 2, 3, 4, 5, 6, 7

20. Areas: 2, 3, 4, 7, 9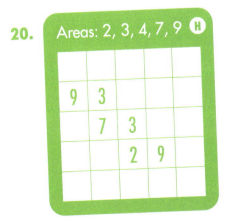

Hints on pages 170-171

FILLOMINOES

☆ ☆ ★ ★ ★

21. Areas: 3, 4, 5, 6, 7 H

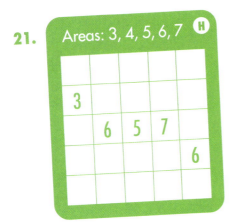

22. Areas: 4, 5, 6, 7 H

23. Areas: 3, 5, 7, 9 H

24. Areas: 1, 2, 3, 5, 6, 8 H

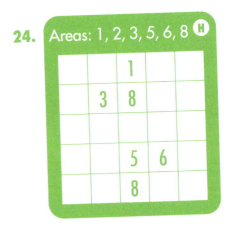

25. Areas: 1, 2, 3, 4, 5, 6 H

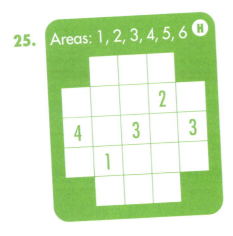

26. Areas: 4, 5, 6, 7, 8 H

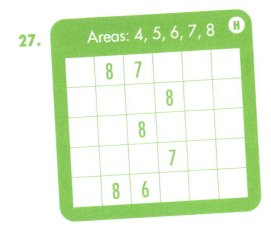

27. Areas: 4, 5, 6, 7, 8

28. Areas: 4, 5, 7, 8, 10

29. Areas: 3, 4, 7, 8, 9

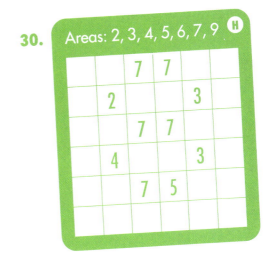

30. Areas: 2, 3, 4, 5, 6, 7, 9

31. Areas: 5, 7, 9, 11

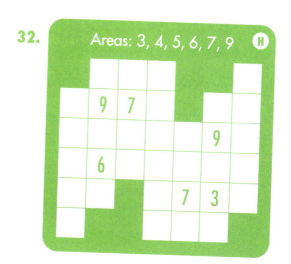

32. Areas: 3, 4, 5, 6, 7, 9

Hints on pages 170-171

33. Areas: 2, 3, 4, 5, 12, 15 **H**

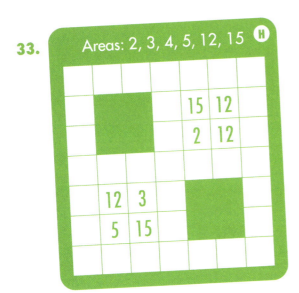

34. Areas: 4, 5, 6, 7, 8, 9 **H**

35. Areas: 4, 6, 8, 10, 12 **H**

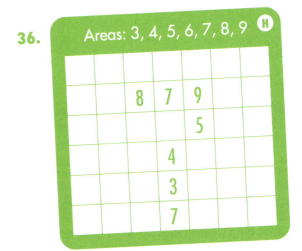

36. Areas: 3, 4, 5, 6, 7, 8, 9 **H**

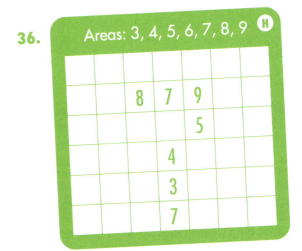

37. Areas: 2, 3, 4, 5, 6, 8, 9 **H**

38. Areas: 3, 5, 7, 11, 15 **H**

39. Areas: 2, 4, 6, 8, 10

40. Areas: 3, 4, 6, 7, 9, 10

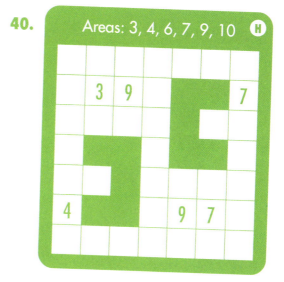

41. Areas: 6, 8, 10, 12

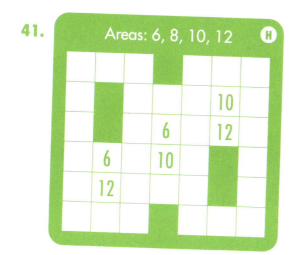

42. Areas: 4, 5, 6, 7, 9

43. Areas: 2, 3, 5, 7, 11, 13

44. Areas: 1, 3, 5, 7, 9, 11, 13

Hints on pages 170-171

45.

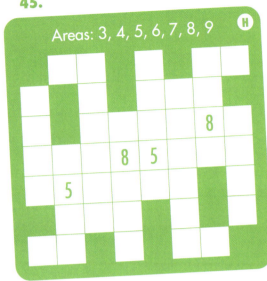

Areas: 3, 4, 5, 6, 7, 8, 9

46.

Areas: 3, 6, 9, 12, 15

47.

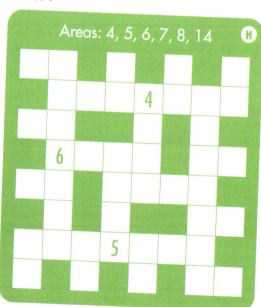

Areas: 4, 5, 6, 7, 8, 14

48.

Areas: 4, 6, 7, 9, 10, 12

49.

Areas: 5, 6, 8, 9, 10, 11 (H)

		10			
			5		
6				5	
		8			10
			9		10
				8	
				9	

50.

Areas: 3, 5, 7, 9, 11, 13 (H)

			7		13
		3			11
11					11
		13		7	

51.

Areas: 3, 4, 5, 6, 8, 9, 13, 16 (H)

				4		
			8			
9		9		4		
		8			16	
			3			16
			3		5	5
				6		
				6		

52.

Areas: 2, 3, 4, 5, 6, 7, 8, 9, 12 (H)

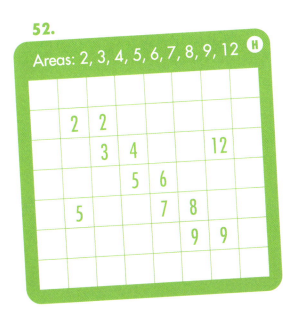

FILLOMINOES
STRATEGIES

1. Cross out numbers from the list when completing polyominoes.

As we complete polyominoes, we can cross them out from the given list.

Also, mark which polyominoes don't have any starting numbers in the grid.

2. Find polyominoes that can only be completed in one way.

How can we complete the 5-omino?

Areas: 3, 4, 5

All the squares of the 5-omino must touch. There is only one empty square touching the 5, so we place a 5 in this square.

Then, there is only one empty square touching this 5, so we also place a 5 there.

We continue this way until the 5-omino is complete.

(Sometimes we can only complete part of the polyomino. That's still useful.)

3. Find polyominoes that can only fit in one region.

Where can we place the 6-omino?

Areas: 1, 2, 3, 6

In the top-left empty part of the grid, there are three empty squares. In the bottom-right empty part of the grid, there are six empty squares.

So, we can only place the 6-omino in the bottom-right region of the grid.

(This strategy is helpful when placing polyominoes that have no starting number on the grid.)

4. Don't isolate regions that can't be filled.

How can we complete the 4-omino?

Areas: 2, 4, 6

We need two more squares to complete the 4-omino. There are two ways to connect the two existing 4's:

However, if we place the 4's as shown on the left, there is one empty square in the top-right corner. Since there is no polyomino with area 1, we could never fill this square.

So, we place the 4's as shown.

5. Find squares that can only be part of one polyomino.

Sometimes, an empty square (often in a distant corner) can only be part of one polyomino.

Which polyomino is the highlighted square part of?

Areas: 2, 4, 6, 8, 10

The highlighted square is too far away from the given numbers to be part of the 2-omino, 4-omino, 6-omino, or 8-omino. So, it must be part of the 10-omino.

(Be careful if there are polyominoes that have no starting numbers in the grid.)

6. Find squares needed to complete a polyomino.

If a square is needed to connect two numbers of the same polyomino, fill that square.

What squares must be part of the 9-omino?

Areas: 3, 4, 6, 7, 9, 10

No matter how we connect the two given 9's, we must include the three squares shown below.

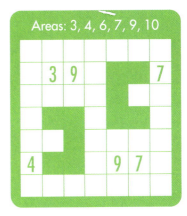

There are still four more 9's to add to the 9-omino, but we must place other polyominoes to find out where they go.

7. Don't block connections.

How can we connect the two highlighted 7's?

Areas: 2, 3, 4, 7

7			2
	4		
		7	
4			7

There are two ways to connect the 7's:

7	7	7	2
	4	7	
		7	
4			7

7			2
7	4		
7	7	7	
4			7

However, the grid on the right prevents us from connecting the two 4's. So, we connect the 7's as shown.

7	7	7	2
	4	7	
		7	
4			7

8. Find squares that must be part of a polyomino.

Are there squares that must be part of a polyomino, regardless of how the polyomino is completed?

What squares must be part of the 6-omino below?

Areas: 5, 6, 7

The square to the left of the given 6 can only be part of the 6-omino. The squares above or below the given 6 can be part of the 6-omino, or another polyomino.

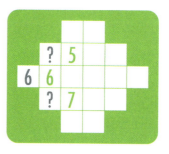

That leaves at least two more squares that must be part of the 6-omino. We can only place these two 6's as shown.

(Now, which squares must be part of the 5-omino and 7-omino?)

9. Make sure each polyomino has enough room.

When placing polyominoes, make sure there's enough room for the other polyominoes to be completed.

How can we connect the 7's?

Areas: 4, 5, 7

7	5		
		4	7

There is only one way to connect the 7's that leaves four squares for the 4-omino and five squares for the 5-omino.

7	5		
7	7		
	7	7	7
		4	7

10. Stay flexible.

Keep looking for the squares that must be part of polyominoes. Sometimes placing just one square of one polyomino will help us complete another region of the grid.

TIMES OUT

DIFFICULTY LEVEL:
★—★★★★

In a **Times Out** puzzle, the goal is to place a given set of numbers in a square grid so that the numbers in each row and column have the product given outside the grid.

There must be exactly two numbers in each row and two numbers in each column. The product of two numbers in a row must equal the number left of the row. The product of two numbers in a column must equal the number above the column.

Each of the given numbers will be used exactly once in the grid, and not every square will be filled.

In this puzzle, we must place the numbers 1 through 6. First, we look for ways to make each product, since each number can only appear once in the puzzle.

$$10 = 2 \times 5 \qquad 2 = 1 \times 2$$
$$18 = 3 \times 6 \qquad 24 = 4 \times 6$$

Since the column marked 10 must contain a 2, and the row marked 2 must contain a 2, we place the 2 in the top-left square. Similarly, since the column marked 18 needs a 6, and the row marked 24 needs a 6, we place a 6 in the middle of the bottom row.

The center column needs a 3. The 3 cannot be placed in the top row. So, the 3 must be placed in the second row.

The top row needs a 1, and since the center column has two numbers already, we place the 1 in the top-right corner.

The left column needs a 5. Since 24 is not a multiple of 5, we place the 5 in the middle row. Finally, the bottom row needs a 4, which can only be placed in the bottom-right corner.

Use 1-6

1. Use 1-6

	4	18	10
24	4		
2			
15			5

2. Use 1-6

	20	3	12
18			6
5			
8			

3. Use 1-6

	18	8	5
12			
4			
15			

4. Use 1-6

	8	6	15
18			
20			
2			

5. Use 1-6

	12	15	4
12			
30			
2			

6. Use 1-6

	12	10	6
30			
8			
3			

7. Use 1-6

8. Use 1-6

9. Use 1-6

10. Use 1-6

11. Use 1-6

12. Use 1-6
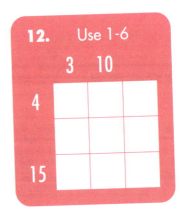

13. Use 1-6

14. Use 1-6

15. Use 1-6

16. Use 1-6

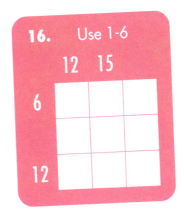

17. Use 1-6

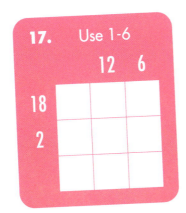

18. Use 1-6

19. Use 1-8

	56	6	10	12
2				
24				
28				
30				

20. Use 1-8

	7	24	6	40
10				
24				
6				
28				

21. Use 1-8

	8	14	18	20
5				
12				
32				

22. Use 1-8

	24	28	10	6
20				
42				
16				

23. Use 1-8

		42	15	4
20				
48				
21				

24. Use 1-8

	12	6		35
21				
12				
32				

★ ☆ ☆
★ ★
★ ★

25. Use 1-8

	2	56	12
35			
18			
4			

26. Use 1-8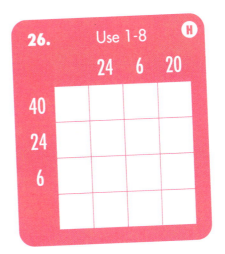

	24	6	20
40			
24			
6			

27. Use 1-8

	20	6	21
24			
6			
8			

28. Use 1-8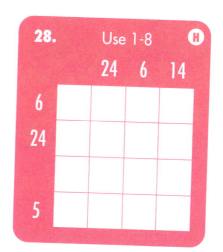

	24	6	14
6			
24			
5			

29. Use 1-8

	24	40	6
6			
8			
24			

30. Use 1-8

	24	8	6
24			
8			
14			

Hints on pages 172-173

31. Use 1-10

	54	10		28	80
10					
40					
42					
36					

32. Use 1-10

	72	12		42	20
30					
54					
28					
10					

33. Use 1-10

	20	16		63	10
45					
20					
12					
56					

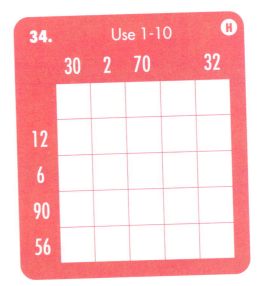

34. Use 1-10

	30	2	70		32
12					
6					
90					
56					

35. Use 1-10

	6	40	42	72	
24					
6					
70					
36					

36. Use 1-10

	10	16		27	20
6					
30					
18					
35					

Hints on pages 172-173   Beast Academy Puzzles 3

37. Use 1-16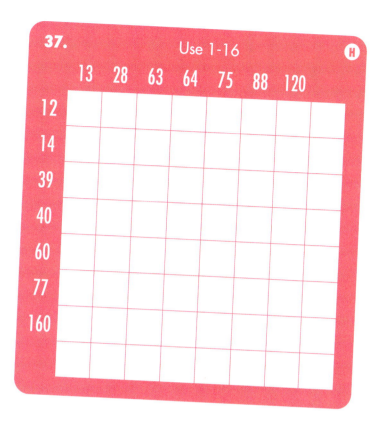

	13	28	63	64	75	88	120
12							
14							
39							
40							
60							
77							
160							

38. Use 1-16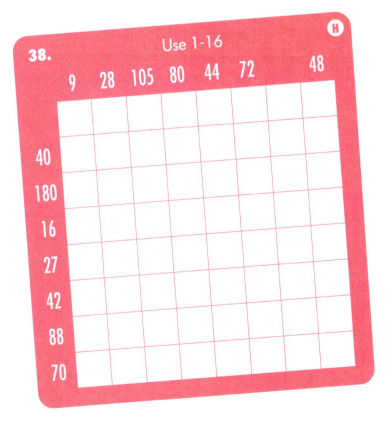

	9	28	105	80	44	72	48
40							
180							
16							
27							
42							
88							
70							

Hints on pages 172-173

TIMES OUT
STRATEGIES

1. Start with product clues that can only be made with one pair of numbers.

What two numbers must be in the left column? Where should they go?

Use 1-6	20	3	12
18			6
5			
8			

The only two digits that have a product of 20 are 4 and 5. So, 4 and 5 must be in the left column.

In the rows, the only multiple of 4 is 8, and the only multiple of 5 is 5. So, we place the 5 and 4 as shown.

Use 1-6	20	3	12
18			6
5	**5**		
8	**4**		

2. Cross out squares that must be empty.

After placing two numbers in a row or column, mark the rest of the squares in that row or column with an X to show that they can't have numbers in them.

Also, if no number can be placed in a square, cross that square out.

Which squares in the top two rows cannot contain numbers?

Use 1-8	2	56	12
35			
18			
4			

In the top row, 35=5×7. There is only one way to place 5 and 7 in this row. We then cross out the other squares in this row.

Use 1-8	2	56	12
35	**5**	✕ 7	✕
18			
4			

In the second row, 18=3×6. Since neither 2 nor 56 are multiples of 3 or 6, we cross out those squares in the second row.

Use 1-8	2	56	12
35	**5**	✕ 7	✕
18	✕	✕	
4			

3. Find the only square a number can fill.

Where must we place the 6?

Use 1-6	8		3
18			
10			
4			

In the rows, the only multiple of 6 is 18. So, 6 must go in the top row.

In the columns, neither 8 nor 3 is a multiple of 6. So, 6 must go in the middle column.

So, we place the 6 in the top-middle square.

Use 1-6	8		3
18		**6**	
10			
4			

4. If a number is needed in one row, it can't be used in another.

If there are several ways to make a product in one row, work on the other rows. This may tell us which numbers can't be used in that row.

Which pair of numbers goes in the second row of the puzzle below?

In the second row, either 8=1×8 or 8=2×4.

However, in the third row, the only way to get 14 is 2×7. Since we need a 2 in the third row, we can't use it in the second row.

So, the two numbers in the second row are 1 and 8.

5. Place 5's and 7's.

In a puzzle with the numbers 1-6 or 1-8, only one of the rows and one of the columns will have a product that is a multiple of 5.

In a puzzle with the numbers 1-8 or 1-10, only one of the rows and one of the columns will have a product that is a multiple of 7.

Where can we place the 5 and 7 in the puzzle below?

In the rows, the only multiple of 5 is 40. In the columns, the only multiple of 5 is 20. So, we place the 5 in that row and column.

In the rows, 40, 24, and 6 are not multiples of 7. So, the 7 must be in the bottom row.

In the columns, 24, 6, and 20 are not multiples of 7. So, the 7 must be in the left column.

(In the puzzles that use 1-16, check multiples of 11 and 13.)

6. Look for rows and columns that have the same product.

If a row and column have the same product, the row must contain a different pair of numbers than the column. So, we can't put a number in the square that is part of both the row and the column. We place an X in that square.

Which numbers go in the bottom row of the puzzle below?

We can make the product of 6 with 3×2 or 1×6. Only 3 and 2 go in one highlighted row or column, and only 1 and 6 go in the other highlighted column or row.

So, the square that is part of both the row and the column must remain empty. We place an X in that square.

Therefore, the other two squares in the bottom row must be filled.

In the right column, 4=1×4. So, the bottom-right square must be 1 or 4.

We can't use 4 in the bottom row, so we place the 1 in the bottom-right corner, and the 6 in the bottom-left corner.

Then, the middle column has 2 and 3, in some order.

7. Find all of the product pairs first.

Can we find the pair of numbers that goes in each row and column without filling them in the grid?

In the top row, either 1×6=6 or 2×3=6.

In the bottom row, either 2×6=12 or 3×4=12.

If we choose 2×3=6 in the top row, we cannot make either product in the bottom row. So, we place 1 and 6 in the top row, in some order.

Then, the bottom row must have 3 and 4.

This leaves 2 and 5 for the middle row.

In the left column, either 2×6=12 or 3×4=12.

In the middle column, only 3×5=15. Then, in the left column, we can only use 2×6.

This leaves 1 and 4 for the right column.

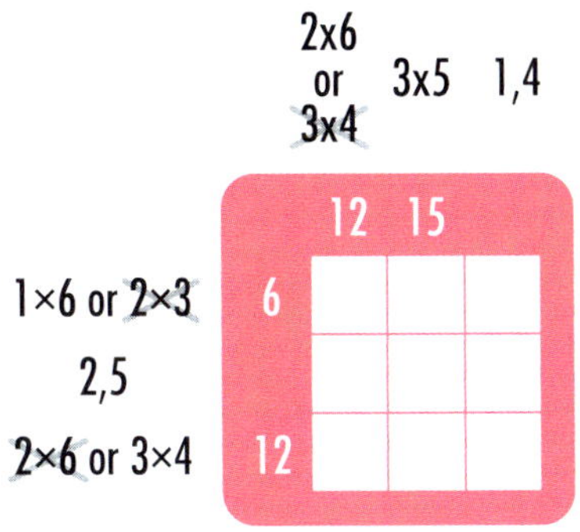

2x6
or   3x5   1,4
3x4

	12	15	
6			
12			

1×6 or 2×3 — 6
2,5
2×6 or 3×4 — 12

(Then, where must we place each number?)

PRODUCT SQUARES

DIFFICULTY LEVEL:

In a **Product Squares** puzzle, the number in each purple square is the product of all the white octagons it shares an edge with.

Every white octagon must be filled with a digit from 1 to 9.

Digits cannot be used more than once in any row or column of white octagons.

Since 5×2=10, the empty octagon above the 10 must be filled with 5.

Similarly, since 9×3=27, the empty octagon below the 27 must be filled with 3.

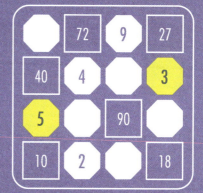

The product of the known numbers around 40 is 5×4=20. Since 20×2=40, the empty octagon above 40 must be filled with 2.

Then, we know 9×2=6×3=18. The only way to fill the empty octagons around 18 without repeating a digit in a row or column is with a 3 to the left, and a 6 above.

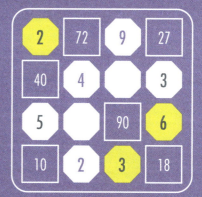

We can complete the puzzle as shown.

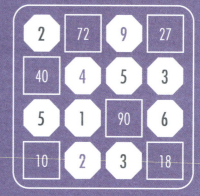

1.

2.

3.

4.

5.

6.

7.

8.

9.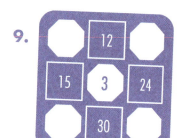

10.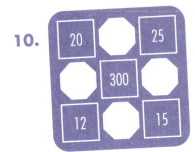

11.

12.

13.

14.

15.

16.

17.

18.

19.

20.

21.

22.

23.

24.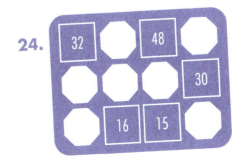

25.

26.

27.

28.

29.

30.

31.

32.

33.

34.

35.

36.

Hints on pages 174-175

☆
★
★
★
★

37.
H

38.
H

39.
H
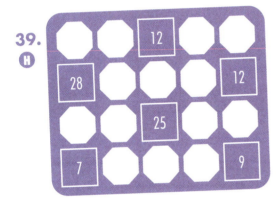

40.
H

41.
H

42.
H

43.

44.

45.

46.

47.

48.

Hints on pages 174-175

PRODUCT SQUARES
STRATEGIES

1. Look for products with one empty octagon.

When a product has only one empty octagon touching it, we can find what digit goes in the empty octagon.

What digit goes in the octagon below the 18?

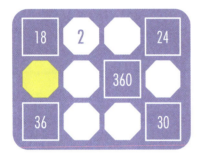

Since 2×**9** = 18, we place 9 in the empty octagon.

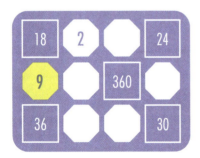

Now, we can use the same strategy to fill the only empty octagon that touches the 36.

2. Consider which digits have been used in each row and column.

Check each row and column to see which digits are available.

How can we finish the puzzle below?

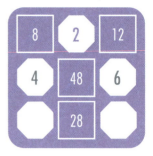

The only two digits with a product of 28 are 4 and 7. Since there is already a 4 in the left column, we place the 4 on the right, and the 7 on the left.

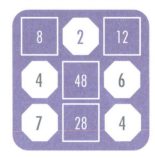

3. Find every way to make a product.

List the ways a product can be made based on the number of octagons touching it. This gives some possibilities of digits to place in the puzzle.

What sets of three digits multiply to 12?

We know 3×4 = 12, and 2×6 = 12. Since we need three digits, we multiply each option by 1.

$$1×3×4 = 12$$
$$1×2×6 = 12$$

We also have 2×2×3 = 12.

4. Look for products that can only be made one way.

Since only the digits from 1 through 9 are allowed, some small or large products can only be made one way.

How can we make a product of 30 below?

The only two digits with a product of 30 are 5 and 6. So, the two octagons touching the 30 must be filled with 5 and 6 in some order.

5. Find products with one shared octagon.

If two products share one octagon, any digit that can be used to make both products can fill the shared octagon.

What digit fills the shared octagon between the products 10 and 5?

The only way to make 10 is $2 \times 5 = 10$.

The only way to make 5 is $1 \times 5 = 5$.

Since 5 is the only digit shared between the products, the shared octagon must be filled with a 5.

6. Find a product that shares all of its octagons with another product.

If all of the octagons that touch one product are shared with another product, we can find information about the octagons they don't share.

Both octagons that touch the 4 also touch the 32. What digit fills the octagon below the 32?

We don't know exactly which digits go in the octagons that touch the 4. For example, we could use 1 and 4, or 2 and 2. But no matter what digits we use, they must multiply to 4. So, the digit that goes below the 32 must be the number we multiply by 4 to get 32.

Since $4 \times \mathbf{8} = 32$, the octagon below the 32 must be filled with an 8.

ARRANGING SQUARES
DIFFICULTY LEVEL:
★ — ★ ★ ★ ★ ★

In an **Arranging Squares** puzzle, the goal is to cover the grid with the given squares. The blue sections cannot have squares placed on or over them, and squares cannot overlap.

The number on each square is the area of the square, and the number next to it tells you how many to use.

Cut out the squares on the next page to help you solve these puzzles.

Cut out the squares below to help you solve the puzzles that follow.

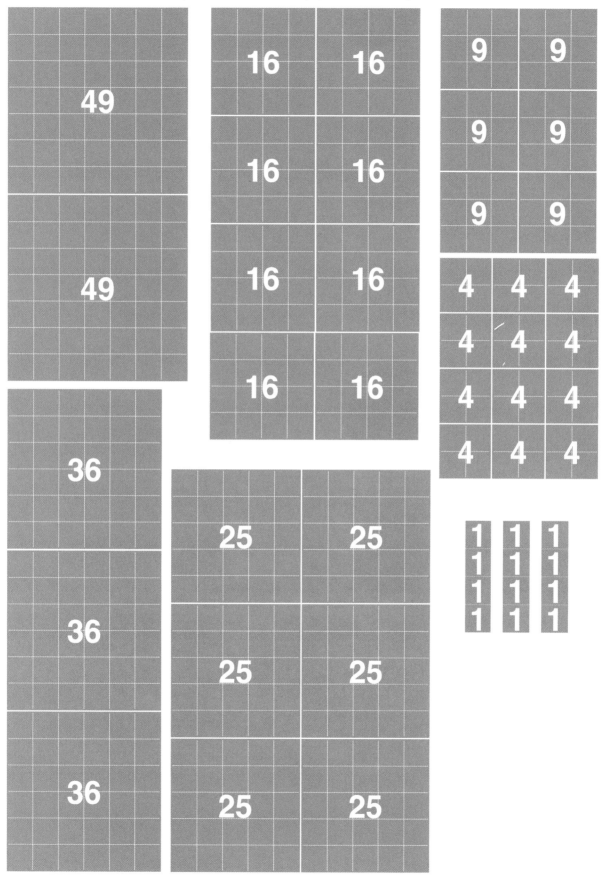

Print more copies of these squares at BeastAcademy.com/Resources

Cut out the squares on the back of this page to help you solve the puzzles that follow.

7.

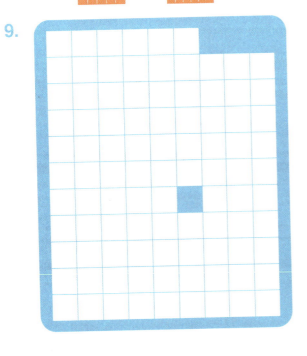

8.

9.

10.

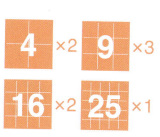

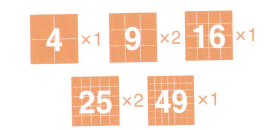

11.

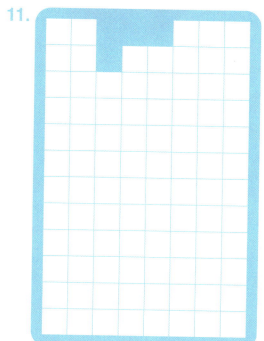

12.

13.

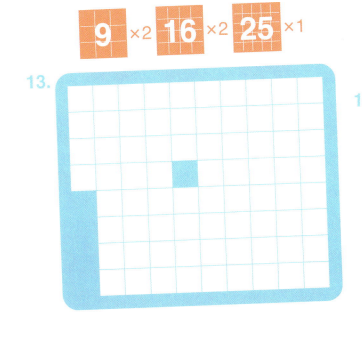

14.

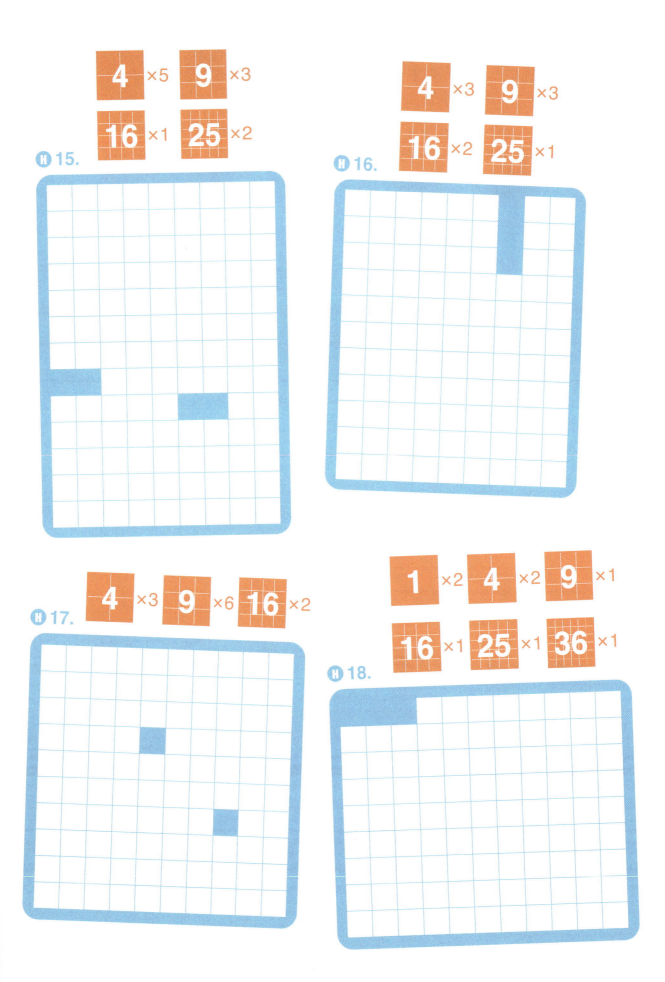

4 ×5   **9** ×3

16 ×1   **25** ×2

H **15.**

H **16.**

4 ×3   **9** ×3

16 ×2   **25** ×1

4 ×3   **9** ×6   **16** ×2

H **17.**

1 ×2   **4** ×2   **9** ×1

16 ×1   **25** ×1   **36** ×1

H **18.**

19.

20.

Hints on pages 176-177

1 ×2 **4** ×4 **9** ×3

16 ×1 **36** ×2

21.

1 ×3 **4** ×3

9 ×2 **16** ×5

22.

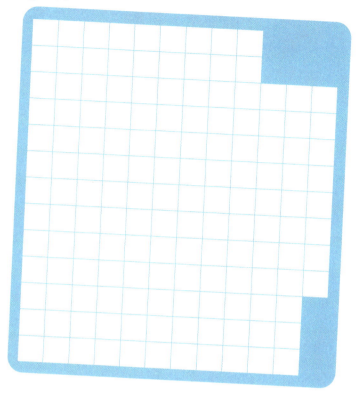

23.

24.

ARRANGING SQUARES

★ ★ ☆ ☆ ☆

Beast Academy Puzzles 3

Hints on pages 176-177

101

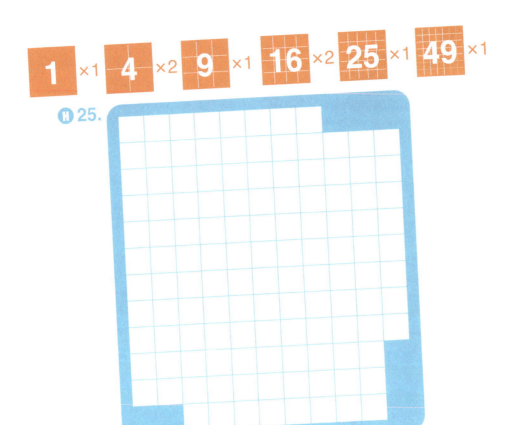

1 ×1   4 ×2   9 ×1   16 ×2   25 ×1   49 ×1

H 25.

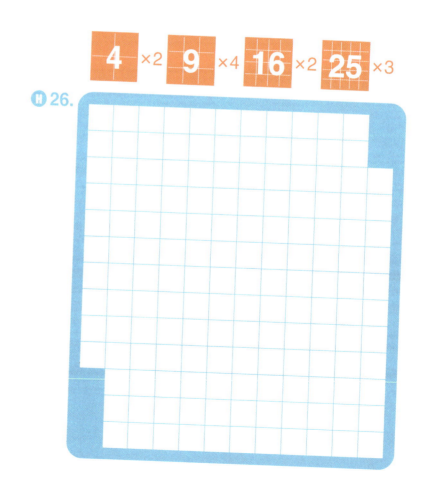

4 ×2   9 ×4   16 ×2   25 ×3

H 26.

★ ★ ☆
★ ★ ★
★ ★

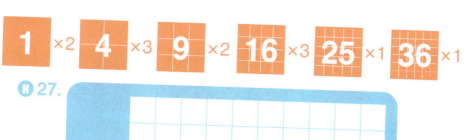

Hints on pages 176-177

1 ×2 **4** ×2 **9** ×1 **16** ×1 **25** ×1 **36** ×2

H 29.

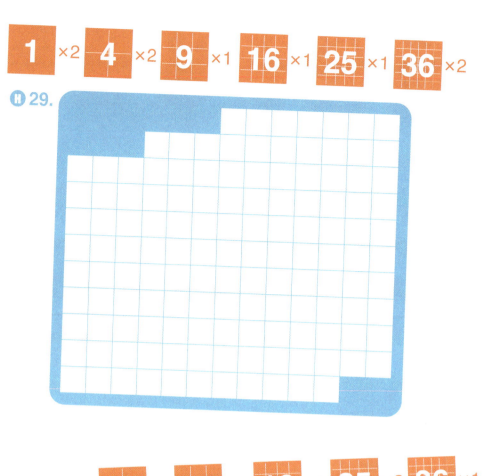

4 ×4 **9** ×4 **16** ×1 **25** ×2 **36** ×1

H 30.

H 31.

H 32.

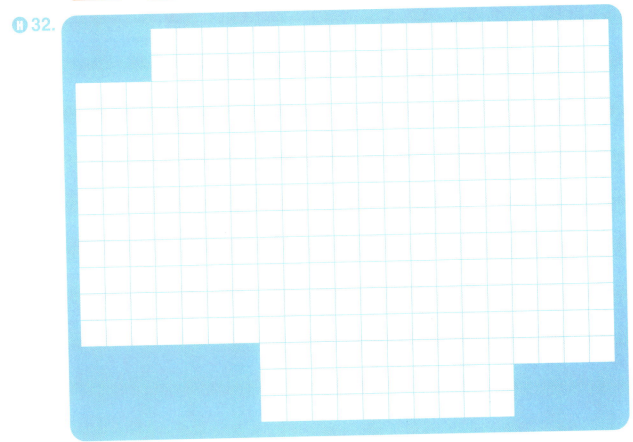

H Hints on pages 176-177

ARRANGING SQUARES
STRATEGIES

1. Find regions that fit one size of squares.

If a region can only fit one size of square, place the square in that region.

What square must go in the bottom-left corner of the puzzle below?

The bottom-left corner has width 2. So, only a square with area 4 can fit there.

2. Start with large squares.

Large squares take up a lot of space, so they can't fit in as many regions.

What square can we place first?

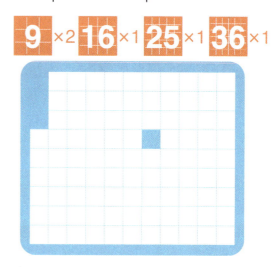

The square with area 36 can only be placed in one way, as shown.

We can continue placing squares from largest to smallest. Each square we place makes fewer possible regions for other squares.

3. Don't make regions that can't be filled.

Don't place a square in a way that creates an empty region that cannot be filled by the remaining squares.

Where can we place the square with area 25?

The square with area 25 has side length 5, so it cannot be placed anywhere on the right side of the grid.

So, we try placing it in the bottom-left corner. This leaves a single square to its right that cannot be filled using the remaining squares.

We move the square up until it no longer makes a region that cannot be filled.

The only place the square can be moved without creating a region that can't be filled is the top-left corner.

4. Align new squares to existing edges.

Try placing squares so they match existing edges. Blue sections create edges to use, and placing squares creates new edges.

What squares align with the edges of blue sections below?

The blue section in the bottom-left corner makes an edge of width 3. So, we place a square of width 3 on top of that blue section.

The blue section in the bottom-right corner makes an edge of height 3. So, we place a 3-by-3 square to the left of that blue section.

Now, the bottom-right corner has an edge of width 5. So, we place a 5-by-5 square there.

We can continue matching edges and using other strategies to complete the puzzle.

5. Match grid side lengths with available squares.

Find groups of squares that match the side length of a grid. Try placing these groups, then use other strategies to see which group will work.

What groups of squares match the right side of the grid?

The right side of the grid has length 7. We organize the groups of squares that fit by their side lengths, making sure not to use more squares than we have.

$$5+2=7$$
$$3+3+1=7$$
$$3+2+2=7$$

We try arrangements of these squares until we find one that works.

(Be careful to keep track of any guesses!)

CIRCLE SUMS

DIFFICULTY LEVEL:

 ★ — ★ ★ ★ ★

In a **Circle Sums** puzzle, the number in each circle is the sum of the numbers in the circles connected directly below it.

Fill in any empty circles and find the value of each variable in the puzzle.

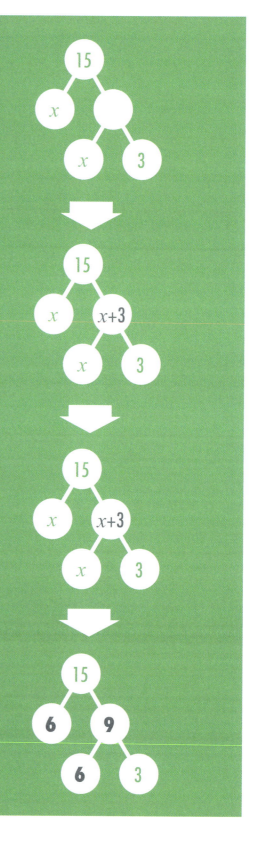

The number in every circle is the sum of the two numbers connected below it. So, we can label the empty circle $x+3$.

Now, we can use the top three circles to write an equation. 15 is the sum of x and $x+3$.

So, we have $15 = x+(x+3)$.

Subtracting 3 from both sides of the equation gives us $12 = x+x$.

Since $6+6=12$, the value of x is 6.

$$x = 6.$$

We replace x with 6 and check our work.

1.

$p =$ _____

2.

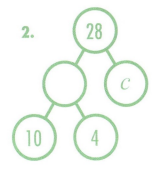

$c =$ _____

3.

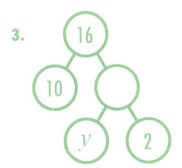

$y =$ _____

4.

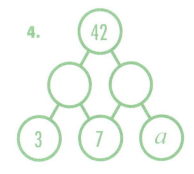

$a =$ _____

5.

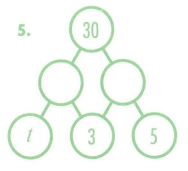

$t =$ _____

6.

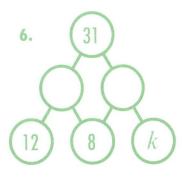

$k =$ _____

7.

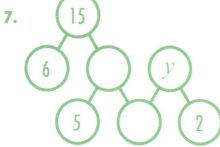

$y =$ _____

8.

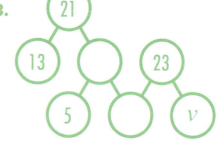

$v =$ _____

9.

$x =$ _____

10.

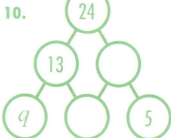

$q =$ _____

11.

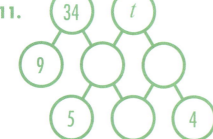

$t =$ _____

12.

$g =$ _____

13.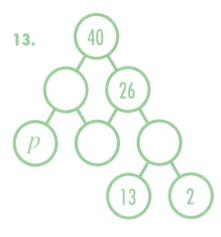

$$p = \underline{\hspace{1.5cm}}$$

14.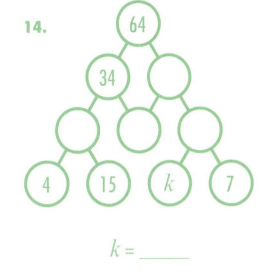

$$k = \underline{\hspace{1.5cm}}$$

15.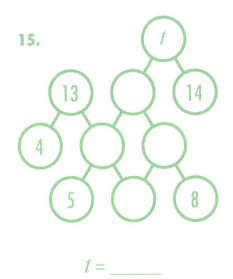

$$t = \underline{\hspace{1.5cm}}$$

16.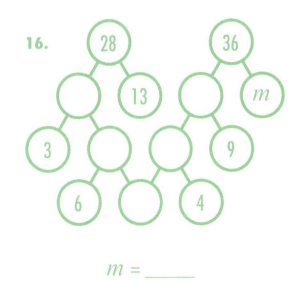

$$m = \underline{\hspace{1.5cm}}$$

17.

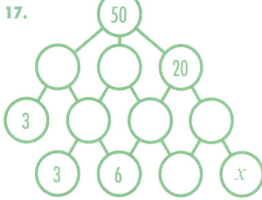

$x =$ _____

18.

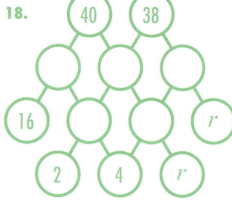

$r =$ _____

19.

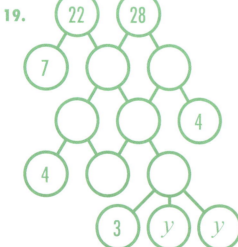

$y =$ _____

20.

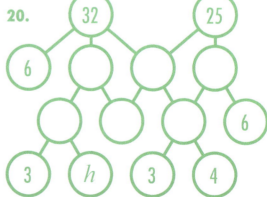

$h =$ _____

21.

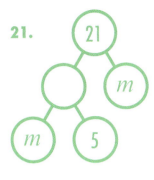

m = _____

22.

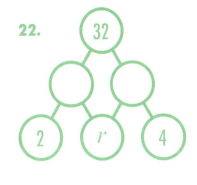

r = _____

23.

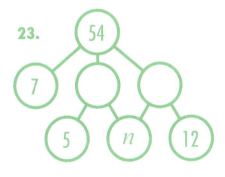

n = _____

24.

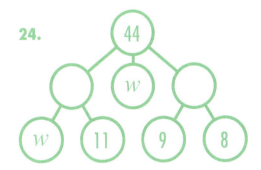

w = _____

25.

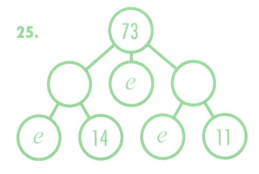

e = _____

26.

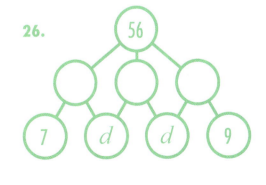

d = _____

27.

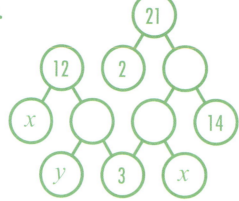

$x =$ _____

$y =$ _____

 28.

$a =$ _____

$b =$ _____

 29.

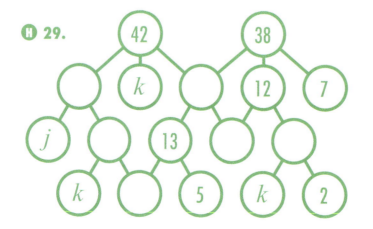

$j =$ _____

$k =$ _____

H 30.

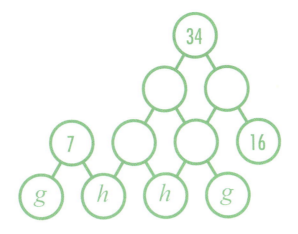

g = _____

h = _____

H 31.

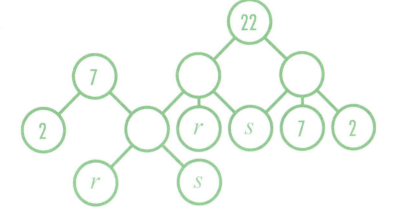

r = _____

s = _____

H 32.

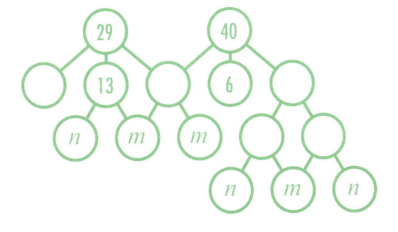

m = _____

n = _____

H 33.

$a = \underline{\qquad}$

H 34.

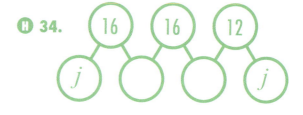

$j = \underline{\qquad}$

H 35.

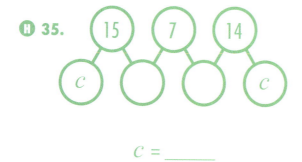

$c = \underline{\qquad}$

H 36.

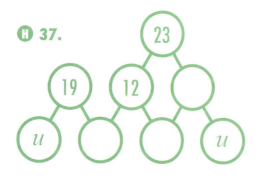

$x = \underline{\qquad}$

H 37.

$u = \underline{\qquad}$

H 38.

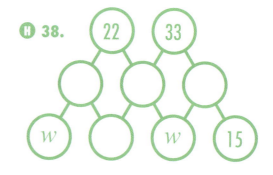

$w = \underline{\qquad}$

☆ ★ ★ ★ ★

39.

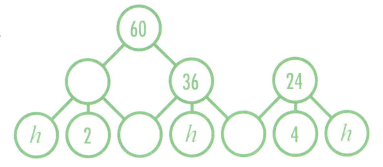

h = _____

40.

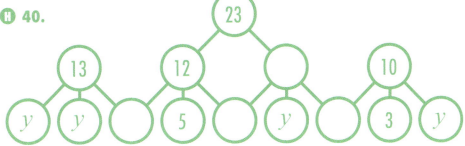

y = _____

41.

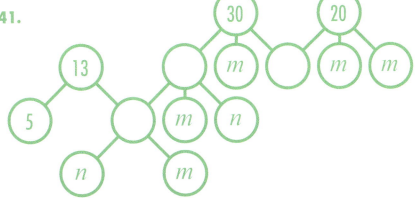

m = _____

n = _____

Hints on page 178

CIRCLE SUMS
STRATEGIES

1. Work top-to-bottom.

If we know the value of a circle, and we know the values of all but one of the circles below it, we can find the value of that empty circle.

What number fills the ●?

We know 13+●=24.
Since 13+**11**=24, we know ●=11.

2. Fill circles with expressions.

If every circle below an empty circle is filled, we can write the sum of the filled circles in the empty circle.

What expression can we write in ● here?

The two values in the filled circles are m and 5, so we fill ● with $m+5$.

Then, we can use strategy 3 to solve for m.

(If a circle can be filled with a number instead of an expression with a variable, use the number! It's easier to continue with numbers than with variables.)

3. Write an equation.

When a set of connected circles are all

filled, we can write an equation to solve for the unknown variable.

What is the value of x?

We can use these four circles to write the equation $4+x+9=26$.

Since $4+\mathbf{13}+9=26$, we have $x=13$.

4. Solve for one variable at a time.

If a puzzle has more than one variable, we can often split the puzzle into parts so that one part has only one variable.

Which variable can we solve for first?

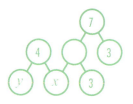

We can split the puzzle into two parts as shown. Ignoring the gray part gives us a puzzle that only includes x. After finding x, we can use the value of x to help us find y.

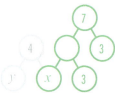

5. Substitute known expressions.

If you know the value of an expression, you can substitute it everywhere the expression appears in the puzzle.

In the puzzle below, ● is equal to $x+y$.

What circle is also equal to $x+y$?

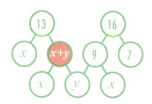

We can use the highlighted circles below to see that $x+y$ is 9.

So, we can replace $x+y$ with 9 in ●.

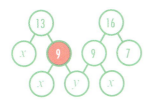

6. Find empty circles with the same connections.

We can compare empty circles that have the same connections.

How do ● and ● compare in the puzzle below?

From the left side of the puzzle, we have $a+$●$=8$.

From the right side of the puzzle, we have ●$+a=8$.

Since $a+$●$=8$ and ●$+a=8$, we know ● and ● must be equal. Since they add up to 10, they both equal 5.

Then, we can use strategy 3 to solve for a.

7. Find empty circles with similar connections.

We can compare empty circles that have similar connections.

How do ● and ● compare in the puzzle below?

From the left side of the puzzle, we have $j+$●$=16$.

From the right side of the puzzle, we have $j+$●$=12$.

Adding ● to j gives us 4 more than adding ● to j. So, ● is 4 more than ●.

We can use this to find the numbers that fill ● and ●.

From the center of the puzzle, we have ●$+$●$=16$. So, we look for two numbers that are 4 apart and add to 16.

Since $10+6=16$, and 10 is 4 more than 6, we know ●$=10$ and ●$=6$.

We place these values in the puzzle, and use strategy 3 to solve for j.

8. Check every circle.

Filled circles are often needed to figure out other empty circles. So, an early error can keep causing trouble. When there is not a clear next step, check that every circle was filled correctly.

FRACTION LINK
DIFFICULTY LEVEL:
★ — ★ ★ ★ ★ ★

In a **Fraction Link** puzzle, the goal is to connect each fraction to another equivalent fraction, whole number, or mixed number by a path.

- Paths may only go up, down, left, or right through squares.

- Paths must begin and end at a number, but they may not pass through squares that contain numbers.

- Only one path may pass through each square.

- Each square must be part of a path.

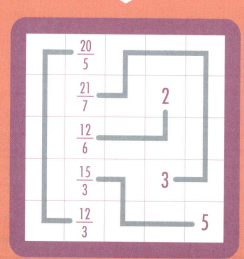

Draw paths to connect amounts that are equal.

1.

$\frac{6}{3}$	4		$\frac{6}{2}$
			2
	$\frac{8}{2}$	3	

2.

$\frac{9}{3}$			2
		1	
	$\frac{16}{8}$	3	
$\frac{8}{8}$			

3.

$\frac{4}{4}$		$\frac{10}{2}$	
	$\frac{2}{3}$	1	
	5		
			$\frac{6}{9}$

4.

$\frac{5}{2}$	4		
		6	
	$\frac{8}{2}$		$2\frac{1}{2}$
			$\frac{12}{2}$

5.

$\frac{19}{6}$		4	$6\frac{2}{3}$
$\frac{16}{4}$			
	$3\frac{1}{6}$		
$\frac{20}{3}$			

6.

		$\frac{8}{4}$	3
	$\frac{15}{5}$		
		$\frac{15}{3}$	
5	2		

7.

	1	2	3	
			4	
		$\frac{40}{10}$		
$\frac{17}{17}$			5	
$\frac{34}{17}$		$\frac{35}{7}$	$\frac{33}{11}$	

8.

$3\frac{1}{2}$			$3\frac{1}{8}$	$\frac{41}{8}$
			$\frac{17}{4}$	
		$4\frac{1}{4}$		
	$\frac{25}{8}$	$5\frac{1}{8}$		$6\frac{1}{3}$
	$\frac{7}{2}$	$\frac{19}{3}$		

9.

3			$\frac{24}{6}$	
$\frac{25}{5}$	4	5	6	
$\frac{24}{4}$				$\frac{21}{7}$

10.

2	$\frac{35}{8}$			
		$\frac{30}{5}$		
$\frac{33}{4}$		$\frac{22}{11}$		
$8\frac{1}{4}$	6	$4\frac{3}{8}$		

11.

3			$\frac{25}{5}$	
	5		$\frac{21}{3}$	
	7	$\frac{24}{8}$		

12.

$\frac{4}{12}$				
$\frac{10}{15}$			$\frac{2}{3}$	$\frac{3}{5}$
		$\frac{15}{25}$		
			$\frac{1}{3}$	

13.

				$\frac{1}{3}$
		$\frac{2}{6}$	5	
	$\frac{8}{32}$			$\frac{1}{4}$
				$\frac{40}{8}$

14.

$\frac{5}{9}$	$\frac{1}{7}$			
			$\frac{10}{18}$	
	$\frac{15}{36}$			
			$\frac{5}{35}$	$\frac{5}{12}$

15.

7		$1\frac{1}{3}$		$\frac{4}{3}$
$4\frac{2}{3}$		$\frac{21}{7}$		
	3		$\frac{28}{4}$	
		$\frac{14}{3}$		

16.

$\frac{9}{18}$				$\frac{33}{15}$
		$\frac{15}{20}$		$\frac{14}{7}$
	2			
	$\frac{1}{2}$		$\frac{11}{5}$	
$\frac{3}{4}$				

17.

				6
		$3\frac{3}{7}$		4
	$\frac{48}{8}$		$\frac{24}{6}$	$\frac{24}{7}$

18.

			7	$\frac{9}{5}$
	$\frac{27}{15}$		2	
		$\frac{36}{18}$	$\frac{49}{7}$	

H 19.

		8	3		
$\frac{26}{13}$			2		
$\frac{72}{9}$					
		5			
	4			$\frac{40}{10}$	
				$\frac{39}{13}$	$\frac{65}{13}$

H 20.

		$5\frac{1}{3}$		$7\frac{1}{2}$	$\frac{54}{6}$
				9	
4	$\frac{16}{3}$		$\frac{15}{2}$	$\frac{90}{30}$	
3	$\frac{52}{13}$				

H 21.

	3	6			
			$\frac{57}{19}$		
			7		$\frac{64}{8}$
	$\frac{56}{8}$		8		$\frac{54}{9}$
			9		$\frac{63}{7}$

H 22.

				$\frac{36}{6}$	
		$\frac{28}{6}$			$\frac{28}{7}$
				6	$\frac{14}{3}$
	$\frac{2}{7}$			$\frac{6}{21}$	
	4				

H 23.

	$\frac{54}{9}$	$\frac{64}{8}$		7	
		$\frac{36}{4}$			9
	$\frac{42}{6}$			6	
	8				

H 24.

	$\frac{63}{9}$	1		$\frac{45}{9}$	
		5	$\frac{63}{21}$		
	7	3			
					$\frac{21}{21}$

FRACTION LINK

☆ ☆ ★ ★ ★

H 25.

		$\frac{15}{7}$	$\frac{23}{9}$	$\frac{7}{3}$	$\frac{24}{9}$
	$2\frac{1}{3}$				
			$2\frac{5}{9}$		
$\frac{8}{3}$		$\frac{45}{21}$			

H 26.

8			$\frac{63}{7}$		
4	$\frac{34}{17}$			$\frac{64}{16}$	
9					
2			$\frac{32}{4}$		

H 27.

$\frac{21}{15}$					$\frac{9}{21}$
$\frac{7}{21}$	$\frac{3}{7}$			$\frac{1}{3}$	
			$\frac{7}{5}$		

H 28.

				$\frac{10}{3}$	
			$2\frac{1}{6}$		
					$\frac{13}{6}$
$\frac{5}{3}$			$3\frac{1}{3}$		$1\frac{2}{3}$

H 29.

			$\frac{38}{9}$		
		4	$\frac{25}{6}$		
	$4\frac{1}{6}$		$\frac{13}{3}$		
$4\frac{1}{3}$	$4\frac{2}{9}$				$\frac{36}{9}$

H 30.

$\frac{4}{7}$					
			$\frac{3}{5}$		
		$\frac{5}{9}$		$\frac{20}{35}$	$\frac{25}{45}$
					$\frac{27}{45}$

H Hints on page 179

H 31.

			7	$\frac{17}{2}$		$\frac{13}{3}$
				6		
			$\frac{35}{5}$			
			$8\frac{1}{2}$		$4\frac{1}{3}$	
					$\frac{36}{6}$	

H 32.

		$\frac{6}{7}$				$\frac{13}{14}$
				$\frac{39}{42}$		
			$\frac{21}{24}$		$\frac{18}{21}$	
$\frac{5}{6}$					$\frac{15}{18}$	
					$\frac{7}{8}$	

H 33.

1	$\frac{42}{14}$					
		$\frac{34}{17}$				
		3				
2	$\frac{13}{13}$					

H 34.

	8					
			$\frac{66}{11}$			
	$\frac{42}{6}$					
6	$\frac{72}{9}$					7

H 35.

	6	2	3	5		
					$\frac{90}{15}$	$\frac{45}{15}$
				$\frac{56}{14}$		
	$\frac{54}{6}$					
	4		$\frac{70}{14}$	$\frac{70}{35}$		9

H 36.

					$\frac{31}{9}$	$4\frac{1}{5}$
		$5\frac{1}{3}$				
			$\frac{25}{9}$			
$3\frac{4}{9}$					$3\frac{1}{6}$	
	$\frac{16}{3}$				$\frac{21}{5}$	
					$\frac{19}{6}$	$2\frac{7}{9}$

H 37.

$\frac{36}{6}$						
			$\frac{77}{11}$	$\frac{56}{7}$	7	
					8	
$\frac{45}{9}$		9		5		$\frac{72}{8}$
		$\frac{64}{16}$				4
				6		
$\frac{66}{22}$		3				

H 38.

				$\frac{3}{8}$		$\frac{1}{7}$	
		$\frac{7}{3}$		$\frac{18}{12}$			
		$\frac{9}{24}$					
$\frac{3}{2}$		$\frac{5}{2}$	$\frac{2}{3}$		$\frac{15}{6}$		
						$\frac{6}{42}$	
				$\frac{48}{21}$	$\frac{49}{21}$	$\frac{16}{7}$	
$\frac{14}{21}$							

FRACTION LINK
STRATEGIES

1. Label pairs of equal numbers.

In each puzzle, find pairs of equal numbers. Labeling each pair with a letter or color makes it easy to see which pairs to connect.

What are the equal pairs of numbers?

We know $2 = \frac{6}{3}$. We color both blue.

We know $3 = \frac{6}{2}$. We color both green.

We know $4 = \frac{8}{2}$. We color both yellow.

2. Find numbers with one unblocked side.

If a number is blocked on all sides except one, we can begin drawing the path that begins at that number.

How can we start drawing paths from the numbers in the top row?

The path starting at $\frac{19}{6}$ must go right, then down.

Then, the path starting at 4 must go down.

Finally, the path starting at $6\frac{2}{3}$ must go down as well.

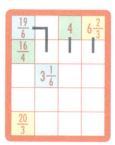

Now, how can we begin the path that starts at $\frac{16}{4}$?

3. Don't block empty squares.

If a square is blocked, it cannot be part of a path.

How does the path starting at 3 begin?

If we start drawing a path to the right of the 3, the top-left corner cannot be part of a path.

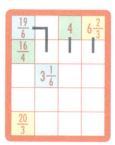

So, we draw the path going up from the 3, then to the right.

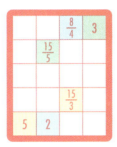

It often helps to follow the edges of the grid to avoid blocking squares and other paths.

4. Don't block a path with another path.

Paths cannot cross. Don't draw a path that makes it impossible to connect a pair of equal numbers.

How can we connect the blue numbers without blocking any other paths?

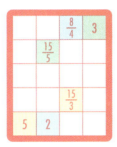

Each path shown makes it impossible to connect all equal pairs of numbers.

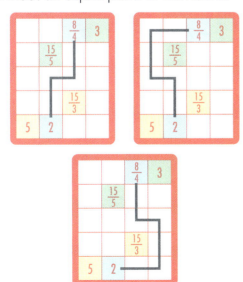

We avoid blocking other paths by drawing the path below.

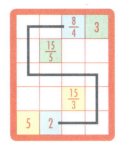

The paths between the green numbers and yellow numbers can now be drawn to finish the puzzle.

5. Use the corners.

Every corner has two unblocked sides. Paths that enter an empty corner must exit through the other unblocked side.

When there is an empty corner, draw a partial path through it.

What partial paths can be drawn below?

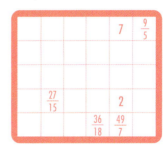

Both the bottom-left and top-left corners are completely unblocked. So, we draw partial paths in each.

The bottom-right corner is also empty. We draw a partial path through it starting at $\frac{49}{7}$.

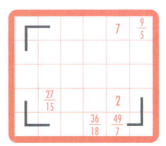

6. Test a variety of paths.

Don't be afraid to guess a path and draw it! An incorrect guess can help us find the correct path.

Which path below is best?

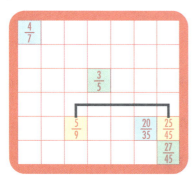

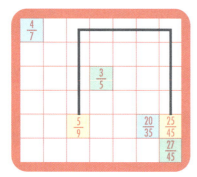

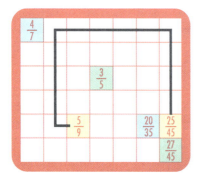

The first two paths make it impossible to connect both the blue numbers and the green numbers. So, we continue solving with the third guess.

ABSTRACT ART
DIFFICULTY LEVEL:

In an **Abstract Art** puzzle, the goal is to shade tiles so the fraction above the grid gives the fraction of each row and column that is shaded.

The top row is already $\frac{1}{2}$ shaded. So, we draw X's in the other squares in the top row to show they must be unshaded.

The only way to shade $\frac{1}{2}$ of the right column is by shading the 1-by-2 rectangle as shown. Then, we can mark the bottom-right rectangle with X's to show it is unshaded.

The third column is $\frac{1}{2}$ unshaded. So, we shade the remaining $\frac{1}{2}$ of this column.

We complete the remaining rows as shown.

1. $\frac{1}{3}$

2. $\frac{3}{4}$
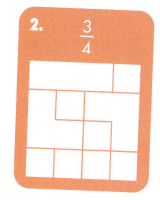

3. $\frac{1}{2}$

4. $\frac{1}{3}$

5. $\frac{3}{4}$

6. $\frac{1}{5}$

7. $\frac{2}{3}$

8. $\frac{1}{2}$

9. $\frac{5}{6}$

10. $\frac{1}{3}$

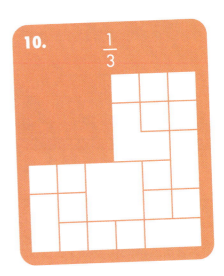

11. $\frac{1}{2}$

12. $\frac{2}{5}$

13. $\dfrac{3}{4}$

14. $\dfrac{1}{2}$

15. $\dfrac{3}{4}$

16. $\dfrac{1}{2}$

17. $\dfrac{1}{3}$

18. $\dfrac{3}{5}$

☆
☆
★
★
★

19. $\frac{1}{3}$

20. $\frac{3}{5}$

21. $\frac{2}{5}$

22. $\frac{1}{3}$

23. $\frac{1}{4}$

24. $\frac{2}{3}$

25. $\dfrac{3}{4}$

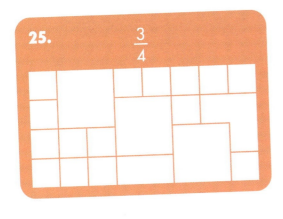

26. $\dfrac{3}{4}$

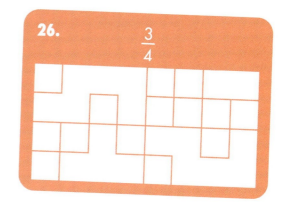

27. $\dfrac{1}{3}$

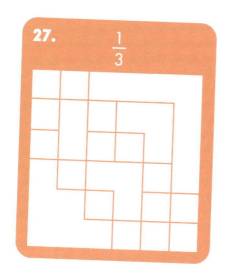

28. $\dfrac{1}{3}$

29. $\dfrac{3}{7}$

30. $\dfrac{5}{7}$

31. $\frac{2}{3}$

32. $\frac{2}{5}$

33. $\frac{3}{7}$

34. $\frac{2}{3}$

35. $\frac{1}{4}$

36. $\frac{1}{4}$

37. $\frac{3}{5}$

38. $\frac{2}{5}$

39. $\frac{1}{2}$

40. $\frac{3}{5}$

41. $\frac{4}{7}$

42. $\frac{3}{5}$

Hints on pages 180-181

43. $\dfrac{3}{4}$ H

44. $\dfrac{3}{5}$ H

45. $\dfrac{2}{7}$ H

46. $\dfrac{1}{3}$ H

47. $\dfrac{2}{5}$ H

48. $\dfrac{1}{4}$ H

★ ★ ★

49. $\frac{2}{3}$ H

50. $\frac{2}{3}$ H

51. $\frac{2}{5}$ H

52. $\frac{1}{2}$ H

53. $\frac{3}{4}$ H

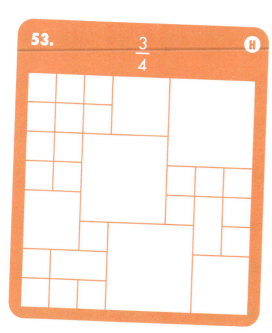

54. $\frac{3}{5}$ H

ABSTRACT ART
STRATEGIES

1. Find how many squares in each row or column must be shaded and unshaded.

How many squares must be shaded in each row of the puzzle below?

In the top and bottom rows, $\frac{1}{3}$ of 3 squares must be shaded. So, we must shade 1 square and leave 2 squares unshaded.

In the second and third rows, $\frac{1}{3}$ of 6 squares must be shaded. So, we must shade 2 squares and leave 4 squares unshaded.

2. Mark the unshaded squares.

Sometimes it's easier to find which squares must be unshaded.

If a square must remain unshaded, mark it with an X.

In the bottom row, which squares must remain unshaded?

In the bottom row, $\frac{2}{3}$ of 6 squares must be shaded, so 4 squares must be shaded. Then, the other 2 squares must be unshaded.

There is only one way to leave 2 squares in the bottom row unshaded, so we mark them with X's.

3. Check large tiles.

It's easier to determine if a large tile must be shaded or unshaded.

Are the three large tiles in the puzzle below shaded or unshaded?

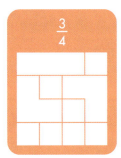

Since $\frac{3}{4}$ of a row must be shaded, 3 of the squares must be shaded and 1 must be unshaded.

In the top row, we can only shade 3 squares by shading the large rectangle.

In the second row, we can only shade 3 squares by shading the L-shaped tile on the right, and one other tile. We don't yet know which of the other tiles is shaded, though.

In the third row, we can only shade 3 squares by shading the L-shaped tile on the left.

4. **Check if we've found all the shaded (or unshaded) squares in a row or column.**

If we find all the shaded squares in a row, then the other squares in that row must be unshaded.

Similarly, if we find all the unshaded squares in a row, then the other squares in that row must be shaded.

How can we complete the third row in the puzzle below? Then, how can we complete the right column?

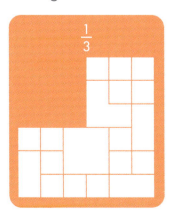

There is only one way to shade $\frac{1}{3}$ of the squares in the third row.

In the right column, we must shade 2 out of 6 squares. Since 2 squares are already shaded, we mark the rest of the squares as unshaded.

5. **Odds and evens.**

If we need an odd number of shaded squares in a row, and only one tile has an odd number of squares in that row, then we must shade that tile.

Which tiles around the edge are shaded?

Each row and column must have 3 shaded squares and 2 unshaded squares. In the top row, we can only have 3 shaded squares if we shade the middle square.

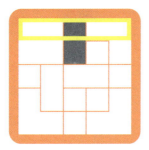

We use the same reasoning in the bottom row, left column, and right column.

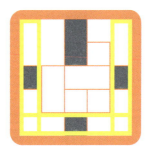

6. Guess and check.

If we're stuck, we can shade a tile and see if it works. Choose a large tile that affects lots of tiles around it.

Is the large tile in the top-left corner shaded or unshaded?

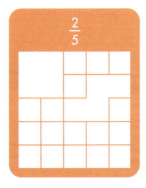

If we shade the top-left tile, then the two rows and columns it's in are already $\frac{2}{5}$ shaded. So, all of the other tiles in these

rows and columns would need to be left unshaded.

But, this makes it impossible to shade $\frac{2}{5}$ of the middle row.

So, the top-left tile cannot be shaded. We erase the marks we made while guessing, then mark the top-left tile as unshaded.

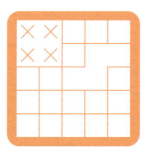

(Keep careful track of guesses, so we can erase them if they're wrong.)

7. Find rows that are linked.

Sometimes the tile connections between two rows (or columns) gives us more information.

Is the top-center tile shaded or unshaded?

In the second row, three out of the five squares must be shaded. So, two of the unknown tiles must be shaded, and two must be unshaded.

All four of those tiles are also part of the first row. Since only two of those tiles are shaded, we must also shade the top-middle tile so that $\frac{3}{5}$ of the first row will be shaded.

8. Switch between rows and columns.

When we complete a tile, it may give new information for the rows and columns it's in. Be sure to check rows and columns as you complete tiles.

SHIKAKU

DIFFICULTY LEVEL:

In a **Shikaku** puzzle, the goal is to split the grid into rectangles so that each rectangle contains a number equal to its area.

Every square in the grid must be part of a rectangle.

The rectangles cannot overlap, and each rectangle must contain exactly one number.

The 3 in the top-left corner is contained in a rectangle with area 3. There is only one way to draw a rectangle of area 3 that contains only this 3.

Then, there is only one way to place a rectangle of area 4 that contains only the bottom-left 4.

We complete the puzzle as shown so that every rectangle has an area that matches the number inside it.

1.

2.

3.

4.

5.

6.

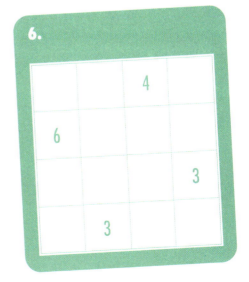

7.

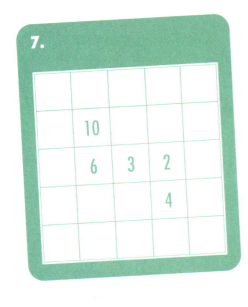

8.

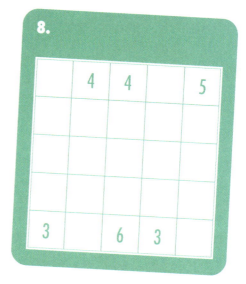

9.

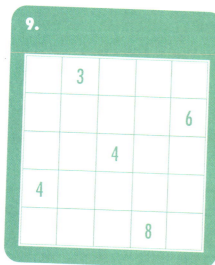

10.

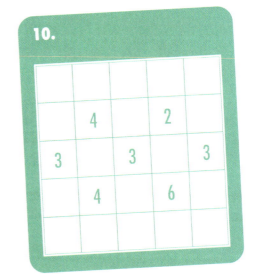

11.

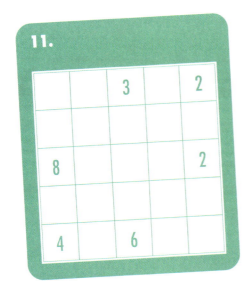

12.

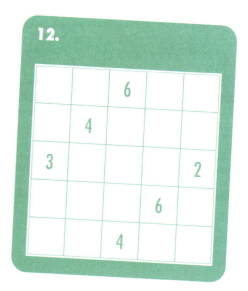

13.

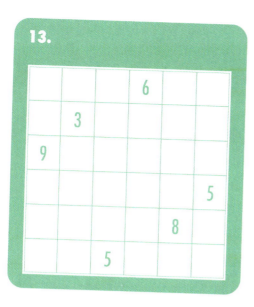

14.

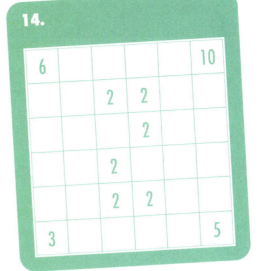

15.

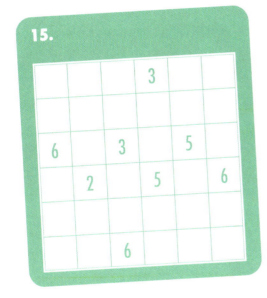

16.

17.

18.

19.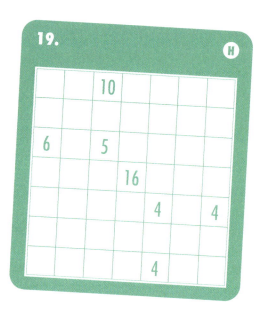

20.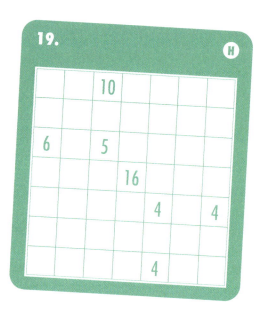

21.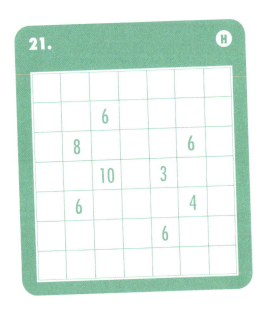

22.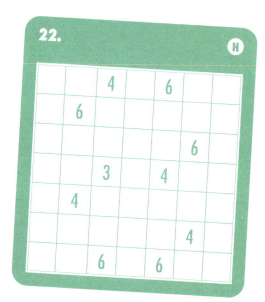

23.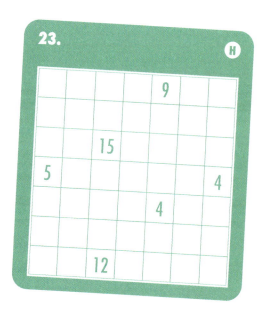

24.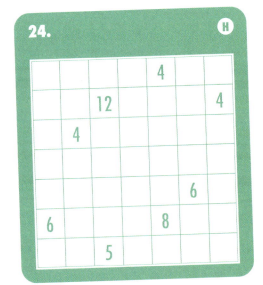

25.

26.

27.

28.

Hints on pages 182-183

29. H

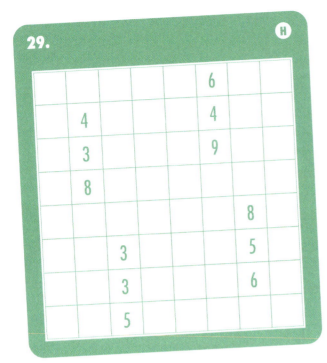

30. H

31. H

32. H

33.

34.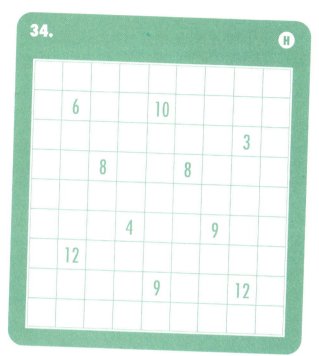

35.

36.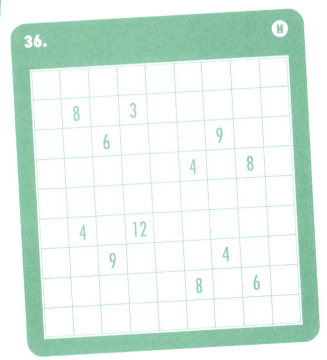

Hints on pages 182-183

37.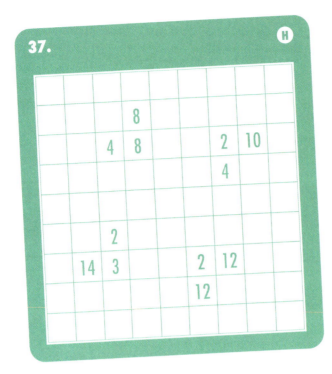

38.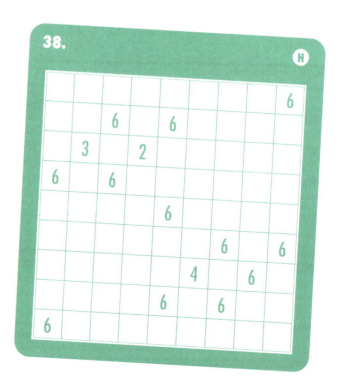

★
★ ★
★ ★
★

39. H

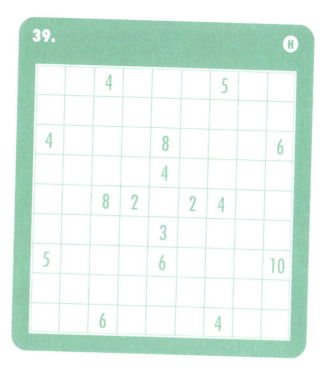

40. H

H Hints on pages 182-183

SHIKAKU
STRATEGIES

1. Consider all possible rectangles for a given area.

For each number in the grid, consider all the different rectangles that have that area.

What rectangles have area 4?

The only rectangles with area 4 are 1-by-4 and 2-by-2. Remember, squares are rectangles too!

2. Find numbers with only one option.

If there is only one rectangle that can contain a number, draw it.

What rectangle must contain the 6?

The only rectangle that can contain the 6 is 2-by-3, as shown.

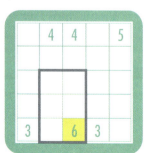

3. Big numbers have limited options.

Big numbers must be inside big rectangles. A big rectangle needs a lot of space in the grid, so big numbers often have limited options.

What rectangle must contain the 9?

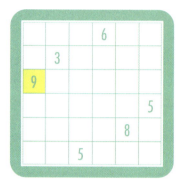

The only rectangles with area 9 are 1-by-9 and 3-by-3.

A 1-by-9 rectangle does not fit on the grid. So, we must place a 3-by-3 rectangle as shown.

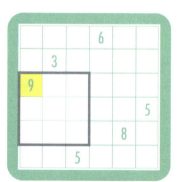

4. Find numbers that can make only one rectangle.

Some numbers have limited rectangles with that area. These are often good places to start.

What rectangles have area 3?

The only rectangle with area 3 is 1-by-3.

So, there is only one kind of rectangle that can contain the 3. We just need to figure out where to place it.

Other numbers with limited options are 2, 3, 5, and 7. The only rectangles that can be made with these numbers are 1-by-2, 1-by-3, 1-by-5, and 1-by-7.

5. Find squares that are hard to contain.

If there is only one rectangle that can contain an unlabeled square, draw it.

What rectangle must contain the highlighted square?

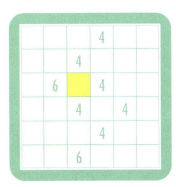

A rectangle containing the 6 to the left, the 4 above, or the 4 below cannot contain the highlighted square without containing another number.

So, the rectangle containing the 4 to the right is the only rectangle that can contain the highlighted square.

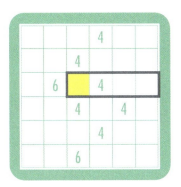

6. Look at corners.

Empty squares in the corners often have limited numbers of rectangles that can contain them.

Which corner below can only be contained by one rectangle?

The top-left corner can only be reached by a 1-by-6 rectangle containing the bottom-left 6.

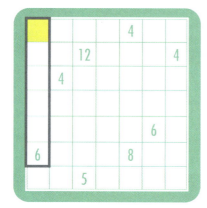

7. Don't block numbers.

Watch out for rectangles that block all other options for containing another number.

How can we contain the 16 without blocking the 10 below?

The only rectangle that can contain the 16 and fit on the grid is 4-by-4.

If we draw the 4-by-4 rectangle below, it is impossible to draw a rectangle that contains the 10.

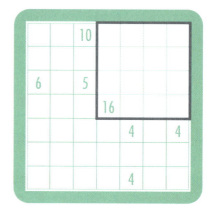

Instead, we draw the rectangle below. We can use other strategies to finish the puzzle.

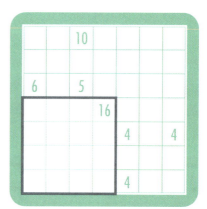

HINTS

HINTS

ANGLE MAZES
(Strategies begin on page 14.)

14. Where is the first turn? The second? There are only a few possible dots for each turn. Eliminate possibilities as you go. (Strategy 3)

15. Working backwards, how can we use four consecutive obtuse angles? (Strategy 2)

16. What could a path with the pattern acute-obtuse-obtuse look like? (Strategies 4, 5)

17. The final turn of the path must be in the top row. How can the path get there? (Strategy 2)

18. What could a path with three acute angles look like? (Strategy 5)

19. Where is the first turn? The second? There are only a few possible dots for each turn. Eliminate possibilities as you go. (Strategy 3)

20. Work backwards. Is it easier for the path to go to the left or to the right of the maze's central hole? (Strategies 2, 3)

21. Which right angles are in the maze? (Strategy 4)

22. Which right angles are in the maze? Can you draw the beginning and end of the path? (Strategy 4)

23. Which right angles are in the maze? (Strategy 4)

24. Work backwards. Which right angles are in the maze? (Strategies 2, 4)

25. Turning only acute angles can give a zig-zag pattern if you turn one way then the other, or a star-like pattern if you always turn the same way. Which works better here? (Strategy 5)

26. There are not many ways to begin the path with an acute turn followed by an obtuse turn. There are not many ways to end the path with the angles given. Try drawing the start and the end and look for a way to connect them. (Strategies 2, 4)

27. Working backwards, there are only two ways to end the path obtuse-obtuse-right. Which of these works? (Strategies 2, 3)

28. Working backwards, what paths have three consecutive obtuse angles? (Strategies 2, 4)

CONNECT THE CRITTERS
(Strategies begin on page 28.)

23. Try placing the piece below so that it touches three critters.

24. In the finished puzzle, the highlighted square below is not covered.

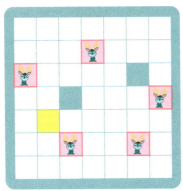

25. Which piece can connect the highlighted critter to another critter?

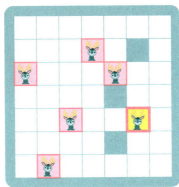

26. One piece touches the two critters highlighted below.

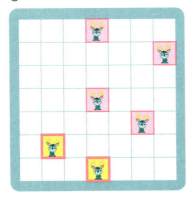

27. Which piece can we place that can touch three critters?

28. Where can we place the piece below? (Strategy 4)

29. One piece connects the two critters highlighted below.

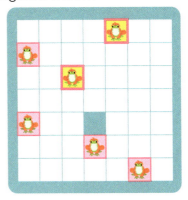

30. Try placing the piece below so that it touches three critters.

31. Which side of the highlighted critter can have a piece touching it?

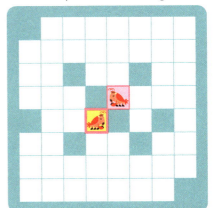

32. One piece touches the two critters highlighted below.

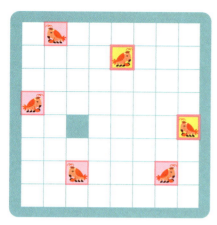

33. In the finished puzzle, the highlighted square below is not covered.

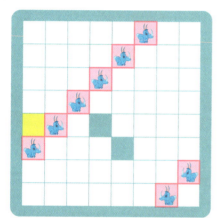

34. In the finished puzzle, the highlighted square below is not covered.

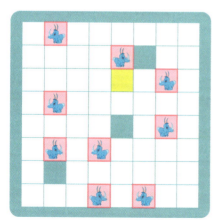

Beast Academy Puzzles 3 - Hints

SKIP-COUNTING PATHS
(Strategies begin on page 38.)

16. Which other number must be part of the path that includes 15? (Strategies 2, 5)

17. How can you connect the 3 to the 6 without blocking another path? (Strategy 6)

18. Which path is 80 part of? (Strategies 1, 6)

19. Which path can the 26 be part of? (Strategy 3)

20. Which path can the 14 be part of? (Strategy 3)

21. Which path is the smallest number part of? Then, which path is the smallest remaining number part of? (Strategy 1)

22. Which path is the smallest number part of? Then, which path is the smallest remaining number part of? How can we draw these paths? (Strategies 1, 7)

23. Which path is the smallest number part of? Which path is the largest number part of? (Strategy 1)

24. Which path is the 31 part of? The 21? (Strategy 2)

25. Which path is the smallest number part of? Then, which path is the smallest remaining number part of? (Strategy 1)

26. Which path is the smallest number part of? The next-smallest? Keep going until you find them all. (Strategy 1)

27. Which path is the smallest number part of? (Strategies 1, 2, 3)

28. Which path is the 45 part of? How can we connect this path without blocking the other path? (Strategies 2, 6)

29. Which path is the smallest number part of? (Strategy 1)

30. Which numbers in the grid must be the ends of paths? (Strategy 3)

31. If the numbers cannot be connected with a single path, would two paths work? (Strategy 5)

32. Which corner number must be one end of a path? (Strategy 3)

33. Which path starting with 12 does not block off other numbers in the grid? Then, which path including 32 does not block other numbers in the grid? (Strategies 1, 6)

34. Which path is the smallest number part of? (Strategy 1)

35. Which numbers must be part of the path that ends at 81? (Strategy 1)

36. Which corner number must be one end of a path? (Strategy 3)

37. Which path is the smallest number part of? Then, which paths are the other non-multiples of 5 part of? (Strategies 1, 4)

38. Which path is the 46 part of? Then, which path is the 44 part of? (Strategies 2, 3)

39. In order to use all the squares, paths must go around the four highlighted corner numbers without visiting them. Then, which path can 45 be part of?

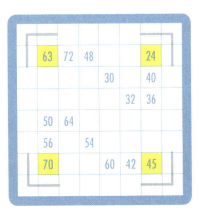

FENCE 'EM IN
(Strategies begin on page 50.)

7. Which  is part of the pen with the highlighted 🦑? (Strategy 4)

Area: 4
Perimeter: 10

8. How can we connect each pair of critters without creating any isolated squares? (Strategies 4, 5, 6)

9. What pen is the bottom-right 🦑 part of? Then, which pen is the bottom-left 🦌 part of? (Strategy 2)

10. What fences can we draw between critters of the same type? (Strategy 1)

11. Which 🦑 is part of the pen with the bottom-right 🐼? The top-right 🐼? (Strategy 4)

12. What pen shapes have area 6 and perimeter 12? (Strategy 3)

13. Each pen contains two animals and one empty square. How can each empty square be part of a pen? (Strategy 5)

14. Which 🐰 is part of the pen with the 🐸 in the top row? (Strategies 3, 4)

15. What pen is the 🐸 in the right column part of? (Strategy 2)

16. What pens are the 🐰 in the top row part of? (Strategies 2, 5)

17. What pen shapes have area 5 and perimeter 10? (Strategy 3)

18. What pen shapes have area 6 and perimeter 10? (Strategy 3)

19. Which 🐫 is part of the pen with the 🦂 in the middle row? (Strategies 5, 6)

20. What pen shapes have area 5 and perimeter 10? (Strategy 3)

21. What pens are the 🐫 in the bottom row part of? (Strategies 2, 5)

22. What pen shapes have area 7 and perimeter 16? How can we draw them while using every square? (Strategies 5, 6)

23. What pen shapes have area 8 and perimeter 18? Then, which other critters are part of the same pen as each 🐊? (Strategies 4, 6, 7)

24. Which other critters are part of the same pens as the 🐫 in the left column? (Strategies 4, 5)

25. What pen shapes have area 8 and perimeter 12? (Strategy 3)

26. Which other critters are part of the same pens as the 🦌 in the top row? (Strategies 2, 4, 5)

27. What fences can we draw? What pen is the highlighted 🐊 part of? (Strategies 1, 2, 5, 8)

Area: 6
Perimeter: 12

28. What fences can we draw? Which critters are part of the same pens as the  in the bottom row? (Strategies 1, 4, 7)

29. Which 🐐 and 🐜 will share a pen with the rightmost 🐛? (Strategies 3, 4)

30. What pen shapes have area 7 and perimeter 14? Then, what pen is the 🐛 in the bottom-left corner part of? (Strategies 2, 8)

31. What pen shapes have area 8 and perimeter 14? Then, how can we draw a pen that includes the bottom-right 🐛, but does not block off other pens? (Strategies 2, 8)

32. What pen shapes have area 6 and perimeter 12? Then, draw fences between critters of the same type. Which pen is easiest to complete? (Strategies 1, 2, 8)

33. Starting with the bottom-left 🐜, how can we draw six "skinny" pens? (Strategies 5, 6, 7)

34. What pen shapes have area 7 and perimeter 12? Then, what pen is the highlighted 🐜 part of? (Strategies 2, 3, 8)

35. What pen shapes have area 8 and perimeter 16? Then, what pen is the 🦁 in the top-left corner part of? (Strategies 2, 5, 8)

36. Each pen is "skinny". What pen includes the 🐛 in the top-left corner? Then, what pen includes the 🦁 in the bottom-right corner? (Strategies 4, 5, 6)

Area: 7
Perimeter: 12

FILLOMINOES
(Strategies begin on page 66.)

15. Where can we place the 6-omino while leaving enough room for the other polyominoes? (Strategy 9)

16. After completing the 2-omino, how can we complete the 3-omino without creating empty squares? (Strategies 2, 4)

17. How can we complete the 6-omino while leaving enough room for the 7-omino? (Strategies 6, 9)

18. Which squares must be part of the 6-omino? The 5-omino? The 7-omino? (Strategy 8)

19. Which polyomino is part of the highlighted square? (Strategy 5)

20. How can we complete the 2-omino while leaving enough room for the 7-omino? (Strategy 9)

21. Which squares must be part of the 6-omino? (Strategy 8)

22. Where can we place the 5-omino while leaving room for all of the given polyominoes? (Strategies 3, 9)

23. After completing the 7-omino, how can we place the 9-omino while leaving enough room for the 3-omino? (Strategies 2, 9)

24. How can we connect the 8's while leaving enough room for the 6-omino? (Strategies 6, 9)

25. After completing the 3-omino, how can we complete the bottom two rows? (Strategies 2, 4)

26. How can we complete the 8-omino while leaving enough room for the 6-omino? (Strategy 9)

27. Which squares must be part of the 7-omino? The 8-omino? (Strategy 6)

28. Where is there enough room for the 10-omino? (Strategy 3)

29. After completing the 4-omino, which squares must be part of the 8-omino? (Strategy 2)

30. Where can we place the 9-omino while leaving enough room for the other polyominoes? (Strategy 9)

31. Which polyomino can the highlighted square be part of? (Strategies 5, 6)

32. How can we connect the 7's while also connecting the 9's? (Strategy 7)

33. How can we connect the 12's while also connecting the 15's? (Strategy 7)

34. How can we connect the 6's while leaving just the right amount of room for the 7-omino? (Strategy 9)

35. How can we connect the 6's, the 8's, and the 10's without blocking one another? (Strategy 7)

36. After completing the 7-omino, which polyomino can the bottom-right square be part of, while leaving enough room for the other polyominoes? (Strategies 2, 5, 9)

37. How can we connect the 4's, the 5's, the 8's, and the 9's in a way that leaves room for the 6-omino? (Strategy 7)

38. After completing the 7-omino, how can we connect the 15's while being able to complete the 11-omino? (Strategies 2, 7, 9)

39. Which polyomino includes the bottom-left square? Which other squares must be part of that polyomino? (Strategies 5, 8)

40. How can we connect the 7's and the 9's while leaving enough room for the 10-omino? (Strategies 3, 6)

41. How can we connect the 12's while still connecting the 6's and connecting the 10's? (Strategy 7)

42. How can we complete the 5-omino without creating isolated squares? (Strategy 4)

43. Which polyomino can fill the bottom-right corner? (Strategy 4, 5)

44. How can we connect the 3's? The 5's? The 7's? The 9's? The 11's? The 13's? (Strategies 2, 6)

45. After placing the 5-omino, and the squares that must be part of the 8-omino, how can we place the other polyominoes without creating empty squares? (Strategies 4, 6)

46. How can we connect the 12's without creating empty squares? (Strategies 2, 4)

47. Which polyomino must fill the lower-left corner? Then, which polyomino must include the top-left square? (Strategy 4, 5)

48. How can we place the 12-omino while leaving enough room for the 9-omino and 10-omino? (Strategy 9)

49. How can we connect the 8's while leaving enough room for the 11-omino? (Strategy 7)

50. How can we connect the 7's, 11's, and 13's without blocking one another? (Strategy 7)

51. Where can we place the 13-omino? Then, how can we complete the 6-omino and 5-omino without creating isolated squares? (Strategies 3, 4)

52. Which polyomino is part of the top-left square? How can we make sure each polyomino has enough room? (Strategies 5, 9)

TIMES OUT
(Strategies begin on page 78.)

25. How can we complete the top row? The third column? The second column? (Strategy 1)

Use 1-8
	2	56	12
35			
18			
4			

26. What four numbers are used in the second row and the second column to give products of 24? Then, where does the 8 go? (Strategy 6)

Use 1-8
	24	6	20
40			
24			
6			

27. What four numbers are used in the second row and the second column to give products of 6? Then, where does the 3 go? (Strategy 6)

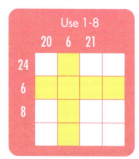

Use 1-8
	20	6	21
24			
6			
8			

28. How can we complete the bottom row? The right column? (Strategies 1, 5)

Use 1-8
	24	6	14
6			
24			
5			

29. What four numbers are used in the bottom row and the left column to give products of 24? Then, where does the 8 go? (Strategy 6)

Use 1-8
	24	40	6
6			
8			
24			

30. What four numbers are used in the second row and the third column to give products of 8? Then, where does the 2 go? (Strategy 6)

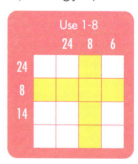

Use 1-8
	24	8	6
24			
8			
14			

31. How can we complete the bottom row? The third row? (Strategy 1)

Use 1-10
	54	10		28	80
10					
40					
42					
36					

32. How can we complete the first column? The fourth column? (Strategies 1, 3)

Use 1-10

	72	12		42	20
30					
54					
28					
10					

33. What four numbers are used in the third row and the first column to give products of 20? Then, where does the 5 go? (Strategy 6)

Use 1-10

	20	16		63	10
45					
20					
12					
56					

34. Which numbers can we use to fill the second row that give us a way to fill the third row? (Strategy 4)

Use 1-10

	30	2	70		32
12					
6					
90					
56					

35. What numbers must be used to fill the bottom row? Then, which numbers must be used in the top row?

What numbers must be used to fill the fourth column? Then, which numbers must be used in the second column? (Strategy 4)

Use 1-10

	6	40	42	72	
24					
6					
70					
36					

36. What numbers must be used in the second column? Then, which numbers must be used in the first column? The fifth column? (Strategy 4)

Use 1-10

	10	16		27	20
6					
30					
18					
35					

37. Where can we place the 7, 11, 13, and 14? Then, how can we complete the third row? The first row? (Strategies 2, 3, 5)

38. In the rows, what numbers give a product of 88? Then, what numbers can we use to get 40? 70? 42?

Can we do something similar to figure out which pairs fill each column? (Strategy 7)

PRODUCT SQUARES
(Strategies begin on page 90.)

25. What numbers go in the empty octagons that touch the 75? How can we place them? (Strategies 2, 4).

26. What number goes in the shared octagon between 21 and 12? (Strategy 5)

27. What number goes in the octagon left of the 35? Then, how can we fill the octagons that touch the 40? (Strategies 2, 4)

28. What number goes in the octagon below the 14? Then, how can we fill in octagons moving clockwise around the board? (Strategies 1, 4)

29. Where can we place the 7 that must touch the 21? (Strategy 2)

30. What number goes in the highlighted octagon? Then, how must we fill the octagons that touch the 16? (Strategies 2, 6)

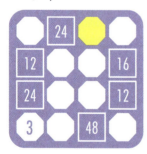

31. After using Strategy 1, how must we fill the octagons that touch the 75? (Strategies 1, 2, 4)

32. What numbers go in the highlighted octagons? (Strategy 5)

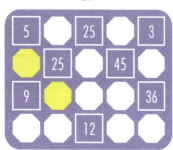

33. How can we fill the octagons that touch the 9? The 24? (Strategies 3, 5)

34. How must we fill the octagons that touch the 49? (Strategies 2, 4)

35. How can we fill the three octagons that touch the 70? Then, how can we fill the three octagons that touch the 8 in the left column? (Strategies 2, 4)

36. How can we use the 4 to help fill the octagon above the 24? Can we use a similar strategy to fill the octagon below the right-most 12? (Strategy 6)

37. After finding what numbers must go in the octagons that touch the 21, how must the octagons that touch the 7 be filled? (Strategies 2, 4, 5)

38. What pair of numbers must fill the empty octagons that touch the 8? The 16? Then, how must we fill the octagons that touch the 9? (Strategies 2, 3)

39. How must we fill the octagons that touch the 7 to make it possible to fill the octagons that touch the 25? (Strategies 2, 4)

40. What numbers go in the octagons that touch the 10? The 75? (Strategies 2, 4)

41. What is the product of the octagons shared by the 10 and 20? Then, what number goes in the octagon below the 10? Use a similar strategy with the 12 and the 24. (Strategy 6)

42. How must we fill the empty octagons that touch the 21? Then, how can we fill the empty octagons that touch the right-most 12? (Strategies 2, 4)

43. How must we fill the octagons that touch the top-right 35? The top-left 35? (Strategies 2, 4)

44. What number goes in the bottom-left octagon? The top-right octagon? (Strategy 5)

45. What number goes in the octagon shared by 30 and 40? By 10 and 56? What numbers go in the octagons shared by 60 and 70? (Strategies 2, 5)

46. How must we fill the octagons that touch the 24? (Strategies 2, 3)

47. How must we fill the octagons that touch the 20? The 56? (Strategies 3, 5)

48. How must we fill the octagons that touch the 36 and 32? (Strategies 3, 5)

ARRANGING SQUARES
(Strategies begin on page 106.)

15. How can we fill the bottom-left corner without creating unfillable regions? (Strategy 3)

16. How must we fill the top-right corner? How can we fill the top-left corner with the remaining squares? (Strategies 1, 3)

17. Which square best fills the top-left corner? Then, which square goes to its right? (Strategies 3, 4)

18. How can the squares with areas 25 and 36 be placed to leave room for the square with area 16? (Strategy 3)

19. Where can we place the first square with area 25? (Strategy 4)

20. What groups of squares fit along the bottom row? (Strategy 5)

21. What square can we align with the top section of the right edge? Then, what square can we place in the top-left corner? (Strategy 4)

22. The bottom section of the left edge has length 8. What groups of squares fit along that edge? (Strategy 5)

23. After aligning squares along the highlighted edges, what square goes in the middle section of the right edge? (Strategy 4)

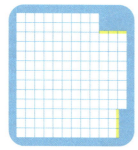

24. How can we align squares with each section of the top edge? (Strategy 4)

25. How can we place the square with area 49 without creating unfillable regions? (Strategy 3)

26. How can we align squares in the top-right and bottom-left corners? Then, where can we place the squares with area 25 without creating unfillable regions? (Strategies 3, 4)

27. The bottom edge has length 8. How can we fill it with only 2 squares? (Strategy 5)

28. After aligning squares along the highlighted edges, what are some ways we can place the square with area 36? (Strategies 2, 4)

29. How can we place both squares with area 36 without creating unfillable regions? (Strategies 2, 3)

30. How can we place 2 squares along the right edge of length 10? (Strategy 5)

31. After aligning squares along the highlighted edges, how can we fill the left and right edges? (Strategies 4, 5)

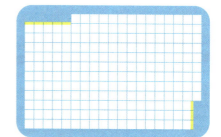

32. After aligning squares along the
highlighted edges, how can squares
with area 36 and 49 fit together?
(Strategies 4, 5)

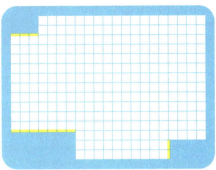

CIRCLE SUMS
(Strategies begin on page 120.)

27. What variable can we solve for first? (Strategy 4)

28. What variable can we solve for first? (Strategy 4)

29. What variable can we solve for first? (Strategy 4)

30. What do we know about $g+h$? (Strategy 5)

31. What do we know about $r+s$? (Strategy 5)

32. What do we know about $n+m$? (Strategy 5)

33. How do the two empty circles compare? (Strategy 6)

34. How do the two empty circles compare? (Strategy 7)

35. How do the two empty circles compare? (Strategy 7)

36. How do the empty bottom circles compare? (Strategy 7)

37. How do the empty bottom circles compare? (Strategy 7)

38. What can we say about the two empty circles below the 22? (Strategy 6)

39. Using the highlighted puzzle below, what equations can we write to help us find ⬤ and ⬤? How does ⬤ compare to 4? (Strategy 7)

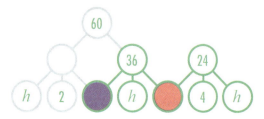

40. After filling in the empty circle below 23, what equations can we write to help us find ⬤ and ⬤? How does ⬤ compare to 3? (Strategy 7)

41. What do we know about $n+m$? (Strategy 5)

Beast Academy Puzzles 3 - Hints

FRACTION LINK
(Strategies begin on page 130.)

19. Where must the path starting at $\frac{65}{13}$ go? Then, where must the path starting at $\frac{40}{10}$ go? (Strategy 2)

20. Where must the path starting at 3 go? Then, where must the path starting at $\frac{52}{13}$ go? (Strategy 2)

21. Where must the path starting at $\frac{54}{9}$ go? (Strategy 2)

22. Where must the path starting at $\frac{14}{3}$ go? Then, where must the path starting at $\frac{6}{21}$ go? (Strategy 2)

23. How can 8 and $\frac{64}{8}$ be connected without blocking empty squares or other paths? (Strategies 3, 4)

24. How can 5 and $\frac{45}{9}$ be connected without blocking other paths? (Strategy 4)

25. Where must the path starting at $\frac{24}{9}$ go? (Strategy 3)

26. How can 2 and $\frac{34}{17}$ be connected without blocking other paths? Then, where must the paths starting at 4 and 9 go? (Strategies 2, 4)

27. Where must the path starting at $\frac{21}{15}$ go? (Strategies 2, 3)

28. Where must the paths starting at $1\frac{2}{3}$ and $\frac{13}{6}$ go? (Strategy 2)

29. How must $4\frac{1}{3}$ and $\frac{13}{3}$ be connected without blocking empty squares or other paths? (Strategies 3, 4)

30. How can we connect $\frac{4}{7}$ and $\frac{20}{35}$ without blocking any other paths? (Strategy 4)

31. How can we connect $\frac{13}{3}$ and $4\frac{1}{3}$? How can we connect $\frac{17}{2}$ and $8\frac{1}{2}$? (Strategy 2)

32. Where must the path starting at $\frac{7}{8}$ go? How can it continue without blocking $\frac{18}{21}$? (Strategies 2, 4)

33. How can we connect 1 and $\frac{13}{3}$ without blocking any other paths? (Strategy 4)

34. Where must the path starting at 6 go? Then, how can 7 and $\frac{42}{6}$ be connected without blocking the path starting at 6? (Strategies 2, 4)

35. How can 3 and $\frac{45}{15}$ be connected without blocking other paths? Then, where must the path starting at 2 go? (Strategies 3, 4)

36. How can $\frac{19}{6}$ and $3\frac{1}{6}$ be connected? (Strategy 4)

37. After connecting the paths starting with 7 and 8, where must the path starting at $\frac{72}{8}$ go? (Strategies 3, 5)

38. How we connect $\frac{16}{7}$ to $\frac{48}{21}$? Then, how can we connect $\frac{49}{21}$ to $\frac{7}{3}$ without blocking any paths? (Strategies 4, 6)

ABSTRACT ART
(Strategies begin on page 144.)

37. After shading the center tile, which tile in the top row must be shaded? In the left column? (Strategy 4)

38. In the middle row, which tile must be unshaded? (Strategy 5)

39. If the rightmost tile in the third row is shaded, what happens in the fourth row? (Strategy 7)

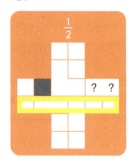

40. Which tile in the top row must be shaded? The bottom row? (Strategy 5)

41. Which rows and columns can we apply Strategy 5 to? (Strategy 5)

42. Is the largest tile shaded or unshaded? Then, looking at the top two rows, is the top-center tile shaded or unshaded? (Strategy 7)

43. First, the tiles below must be shaded for their columns to be 3/4 shaded. Then, what tile in the fourth row must be shaded? (Strategies 5, 6)

44. Is the big tile in the bottom-right corner shaded or unshaded? (Strategy 6)

45. What tiles in the top row must be unshaded? Then, what tiles in the third column must be shaded? (Strategies 3, 4)

46. First we mark the tiles that must be unshaded as shown below.

Next, which tiles in the left column must be shaded? Then, how can we shade 1/3 of the second row without messing up the first row? (Strategy 6)

47. Which of the two large tiles can be shaded? (Strategy 6)

48. Is the tile highlighted below shaded or unshaded? (Strategy 6)

49. The large square must be shaded. Then, we can think of the 6-by-6 grid as split into quarters. How many grid squares in the top-left quarter must be shaded? What does this tell us about the top-right quarter? (Strategy 7)

50. First, we shade the left and right columns as shown. Then, if the highlighted square is unshaded, what other tiles are shaded or unshaded? (Strategies 5, 6)

51. In the middle column, one large tile must be shaded, and one must be unshaded. What does this tell us about the other tiles in the second column? (Strategy 7)

52. What happens if the tile marked below is unshaded? Shaded? (Strategy 6)

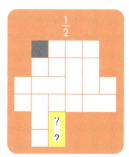

53. Which tiles can be shaded immediately? Then, what is the largest tile we can guess-and-check on? (Strategies 4, 5, 6)

54. Use Strategy 5 to find tiles that must be shaded. After that, what is the largest tile we can guess-and-check on? (Strategies 5, 6)

SHIKAKU
(Strategies begin on page 158.)

19. How can the 16 be contained without blocking the 10? (Strategy 7)

20. First, what rectangle must contain the 8? Then, how can the highlighted 4 be contained without blocking the 5? (Strategies 3, 7)

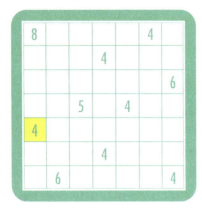

21. What rectangle must contain the 10? (Strategy 3)

22. What rectangle can reach the bottom-left corner? (Strategy 6)

23. What rectangle can reach the square to the right of the top-left corner? (Strategy 5)

24. What rectangle can reach the top-left corner? (Strategy 6)

25. What rectangle must contain the 15? (Strategy 3)

26. What rectangle can reach the top-right corner? Then, what rectangle can reach the bottom-left corner? (Strategy 6)

27. What rectangle must contain the 14? (Strategy 3)

28. What rectangles can reach the top-right and bottom-right corners? (Strategy 6)

29. What rectangle must contain the 9? (Strategy 3)

30. How can the 8 on the left be contained without blocking the 8 in the middle? (Strategy 7)

31. What rectangles can reach the top-left and bottom-right corners? (Strategy 6)

32. What rectangle must contain the left-most 5? What rectangle can reach the top-left corner? (Strategies 4, 6)

33. What rectangle must contain the 10 in the first column? (Strategy 2)

34. What rectangle can reach the top-right corner? (Strategy 6)

35. How can the middle 9 be contained with blocking the bottom 9? (Strategy 7)

36. What rectangle can reach the bottom-left corner? (Strategy 6)

37. What rectangle can reach the top-right corner? (Strategy 6)

38. What rectangle can reach the highlighted square below? (Strategy 5)

39. How can the 5 in the top row be contained without forcing the 6 to block the 10 in the right column? Then, what rectangle must contain the 4 in the top row? (Strategies 2, 5, 7)

40. What rectangle can reach the bottom-right corner? Then, what rectangle can reach the square to its left? (Strategies 5, 6)

SOLUTIONS

ANGLE MAZES SOLUTIONS

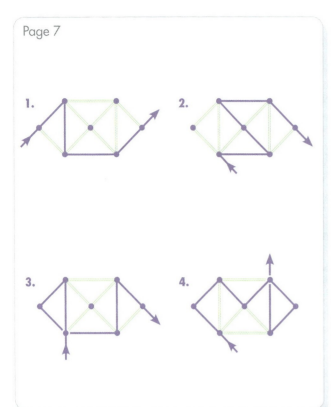

Page 7

1.

2.

3.

4.

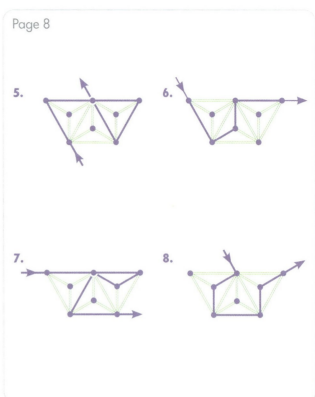

Page 8

5.

6.

7.

8.

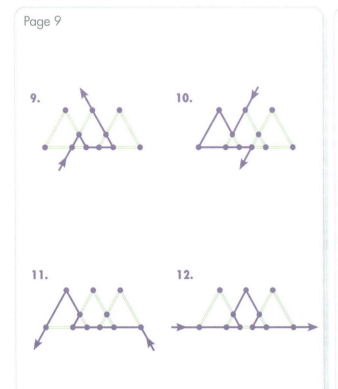

Page 9

9.

10.

11.

12.

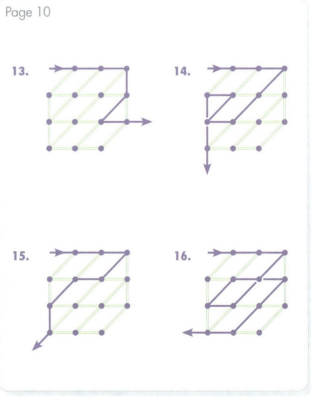

Page 10

13.

14.

15.

16.

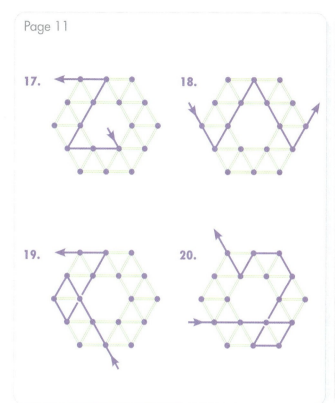

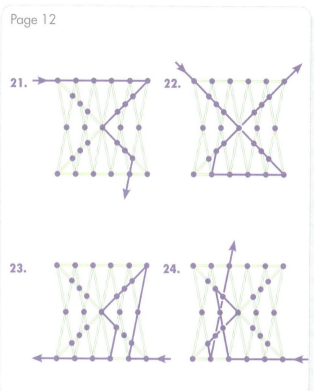

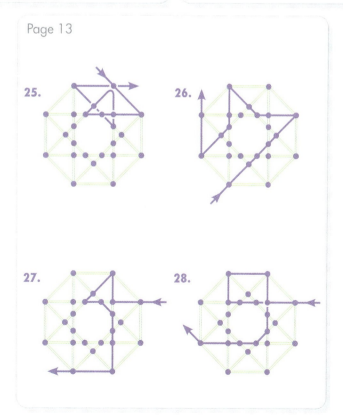

CONNECT THE CRITTERS SOLUTIONS

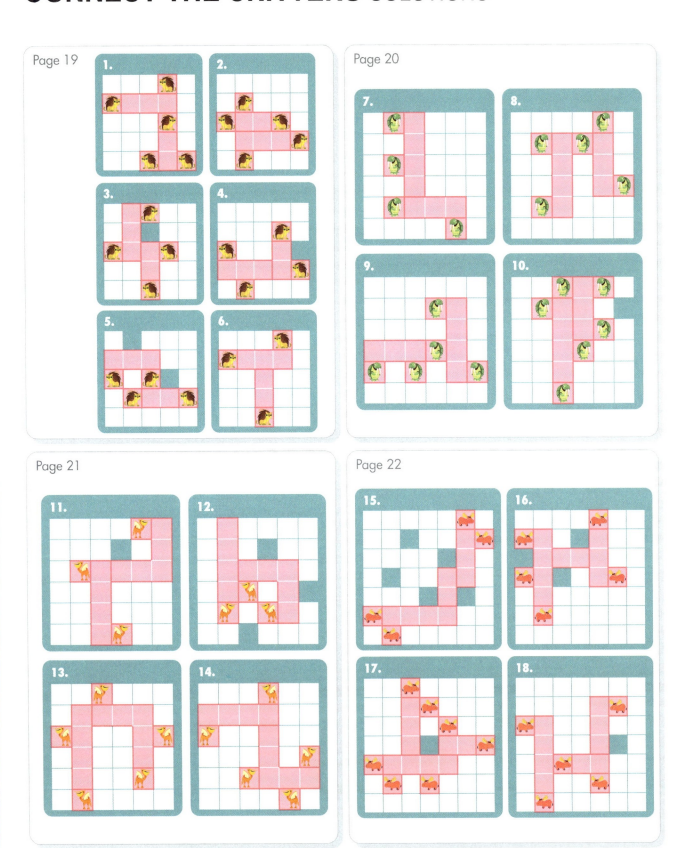

Page 23

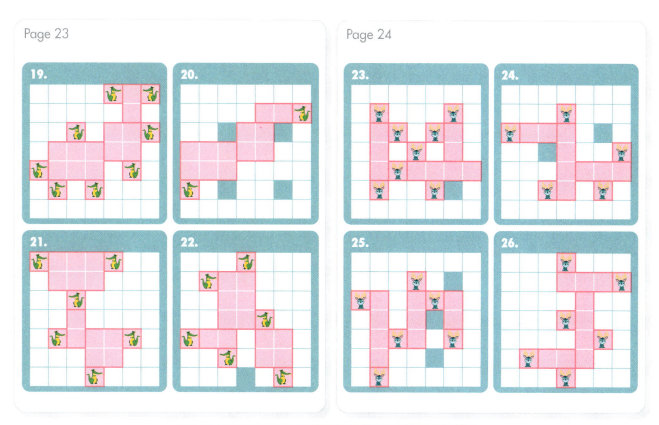

Page 24

Page 25

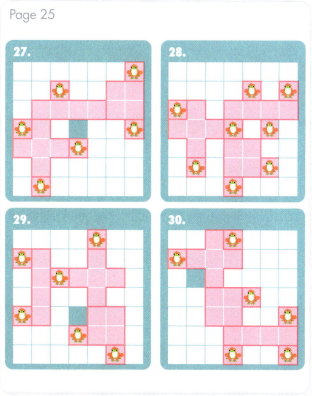

Page 26

31.

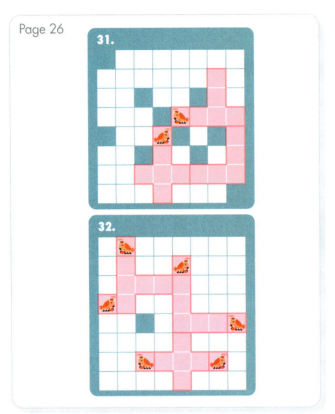

32.

Page 27

33.

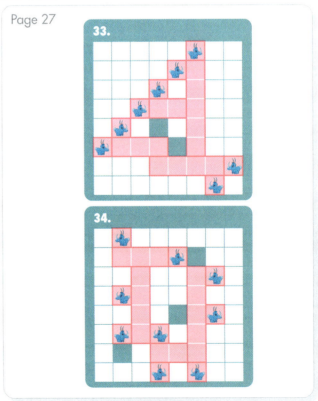

34.

Beast Academy Puzzles 3 - Solutions

SKIP-COUNTING PATHS SOLUTIONS

Page 31

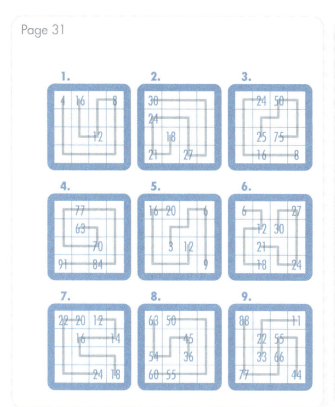

Page 32

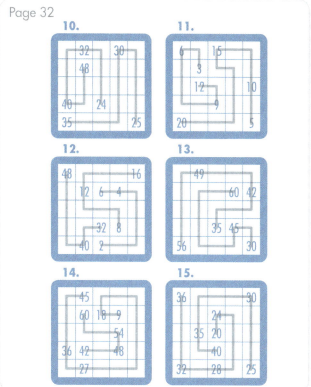

Page 33

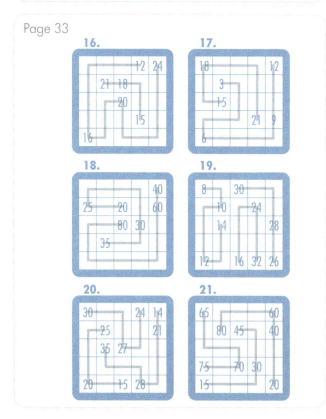

Page 34

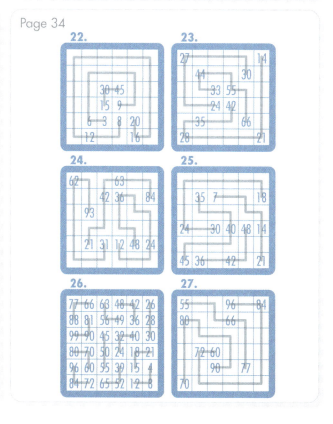

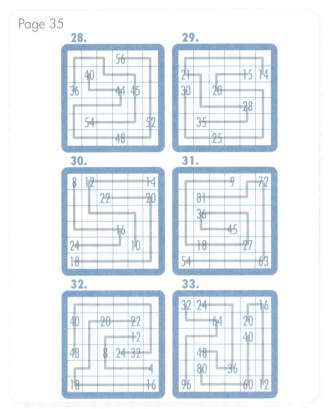

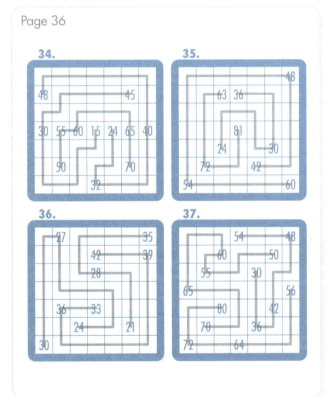

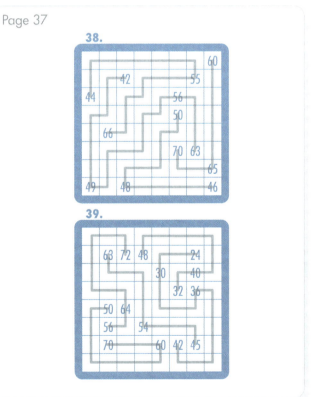

Beast Academy Puzzles 3 - Solutions

FENCE 'EM IN SOLUTIONS

Page 43

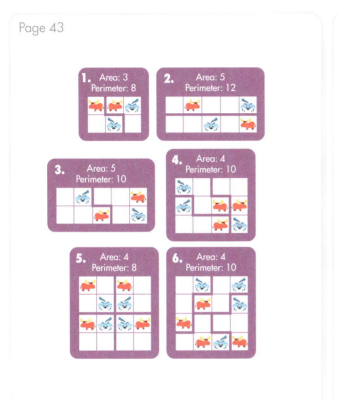

Page 44

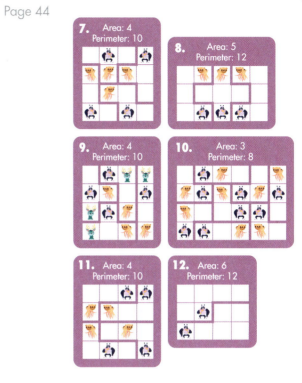

Page 45

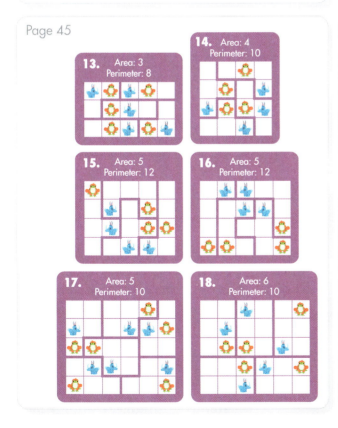

Page 46

Page 47

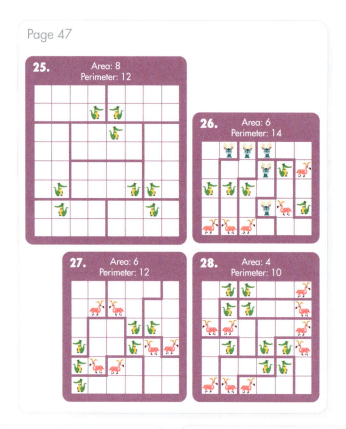

Page 48

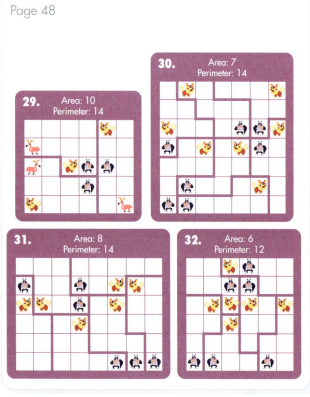

Page 49

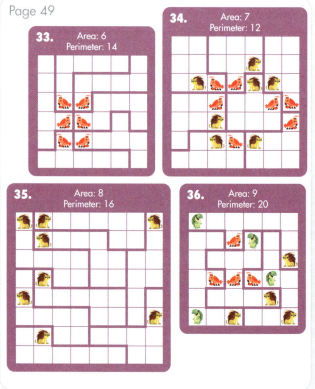

FILLOMINOS SOLUTIONS

Page 57

1. Areas: 2, 3, 4

2	4	4
2	3	4
3	3	4

2. Areas: 1, 3, 5

3	3	5
1	3	5
5	5	5

3. Areas: 3, 4, 5

4	4	5	5
3	4	4	5
3	3	5	5

4. Areas: 1, 2, 3, 6

3	3	1	6
2	3	6	6
2	6	6	6

5. Areas: 1, 2, 4, 5

2	2	5	4
5	5	5	4
5	1	4	4

6. Areas: 2, 4, 6

6	4	4	4
6	2	2	4
6	6	6	6

7. Areas: 1, 2, 3, 4

1	4	4
3	3	4	4
3	2	2

8. Areas: 1, 2, 3, 4

4	1
4	4	2	2
4	3	3	3

Page 58

9. Areas: 1, 2, 4, 5

5			4
5	5	4	4
5	2	2	4
5			1

10. Areas: 1, 2, 3, 4

		4	4
	1	4	4
2	3	3
2	3

11. Areas: 1, 4, 5, 6

5	5	5	5
6	5	1	4
6	4	4	4
6	6	6

12. Areas: 4, 5, 7

7	5	5	5
7	7	5	5
4	7	7	7
4	4	4	7

13. Areas: 1, 2, 3, 4, 5, 6

3	3		6	6
3	2	6	6	6
	2	1	6
5	5	5	4	4
5	5		4	4

14. Areas: 2, 3, 4, 7

7	7	7	2
4	4	7	2
4	3	7	7
4	3	3	7

Page 59

15. Areas: 1, 2, 3, 4, 6

6	1	3	3
6	2	3	4
6	2	4	4
6	6	6	4

16. Areas: 2, 3, 4, 5, 6

6	6		6
2	2	6	6	6
	3	4	5	5
3	3	4	5
	4	4	5	5

17. Areas: 2, 3, 5, 6, 7

5	5	6	3	2
5	5	6	3	2
	5	6	3
6	6	6	7	7
7	7	7	7	7

18. Areas: 5, 6, 7

	5	5
6	5	5	5
6	6	6	7	7
6	7	7	7
	7	7

19. Areas: 1, 2, 3, 4, 5, 6, 7

7		7	7
7	7	7	3	3
2	2	1	5	3
	4	5	5	6
4	4	5	6	6
	4	5		6

20. Areas: 2, 3, 4, 7, 9

9	9	9	9	9
9	3	3	9	4
7	7	3	9	4
7	2	2	9	4
7	7	7	7	4

Page 60

21. Areas: 3, 4, 5, 6, 7

5	5	7	7	7
3	5	5	7	7
3	6	5	7	7
3	6	6	6	6
4	4	4	4	6

22. Areas: 4, 5, 6, 7

5			4	7
5		4	4	7	7
5	5	4	6	7	7
	5	6	6		7
	6	6			7

23. Areas: 3, 5, 7, 9

		9	9	9
9	9	9	7	9
3	3		7	9
5	3		7	9
5	7	7	7	7
5	5	5

24. Areas: 1, 2, 3, 5, 6, 8

3	3	1	2	2
6	3	8	8	8
6	6	6	6	8
5	5	5	6	8
5	5	8	8	8

25. Areas: 1, 2, 3, 4, 5, 6

	5	5	5
4	5	5	2
4	4	3	3	3
4	1	6	6	3
	6	6	6

26. Areas: 4, 5, 6, 7, 8

5	7			8	8
5	7			8	8
5	7	7	7	7	8
5	5	6	6	6	8
4	4			6	8
4	4			6	8

Page 61

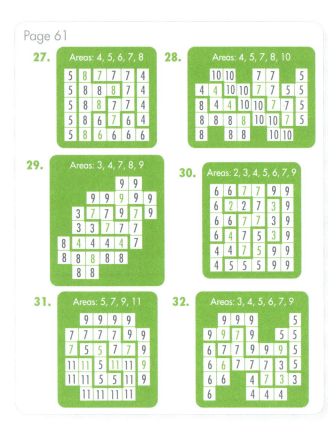

Page 62

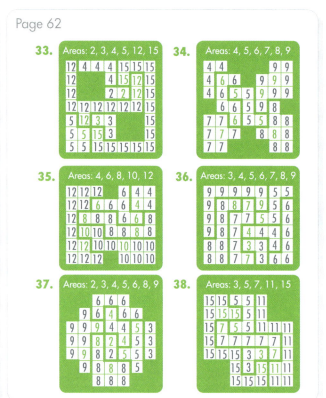

Page 63

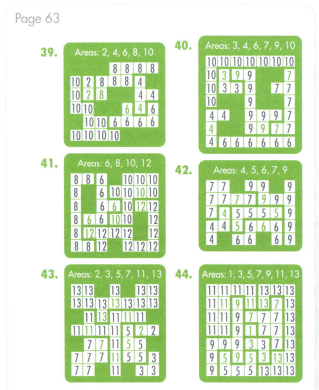

Beast Academy Puzzles 3 - Solutions

Page 64

45.

Areas: 3, 4, 5, 6, 7, 8, 9

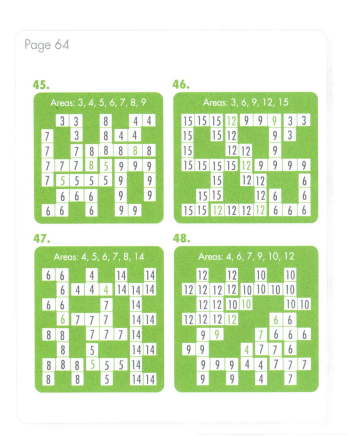

46.

Areas: 3, 6, 9, 12, 15

47.

Areas: 4, 5, 6, 7, 8, 14

48.

Areas: 4, 6, 7, 9, 10, 12

Page 65

49.

Areas: 5, 6, 8, 9, 10, 11

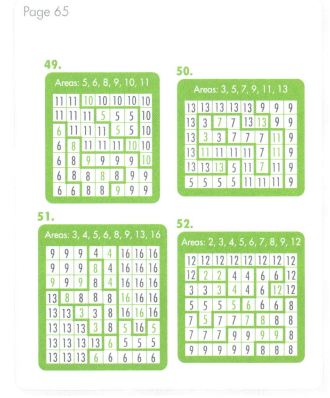

50.

Areas: 3, 5, 7, 9, 11, 13

51.

Areas: 3, 4, 5, 6, 8, 9, 13, 16

52.

Areas: 2, 3, 4, 5, 6, 7, 8, 9, 12

TIMES OUT SOLUTIONS

Page 71

1. Use 1-6

	4	18	10
24	4	6	
2	1		2
15		3	5

2. Use 1-6

	20	3	12
18		3	6
5	5	1	
8	4		2

3. Use 1-6

	18	8	5
12	6	2	
4		4	1
15	3		5

4. Use 1-6

	8	6	15
18		6	3
20	4		5
2	2	1	

5. Use 1-6

	12	15	4
12		3	4
30	6	5	
2	2		1

6. Use 1-6

	12	10	6
30		5	6
8	4	2	
3	3		1

Page 72

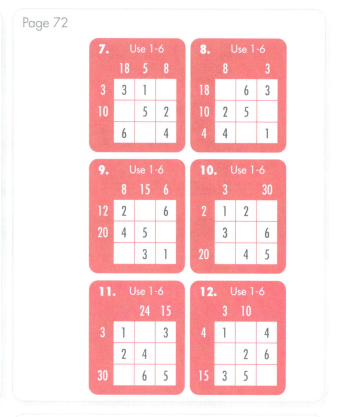

7. Use 1-6

	18	5	8
3	3	1	
10		5	2
	6		4

8. Use 1-6

	8		3
18		6	3
10	2	5	
4	4		1

9. Use 1-6

	8	15	6
12	2		6
20	4	5	
		3	1

10. Use 1-6

	3		30
2	1	2	
		3	6
20		4	5

11. Use 1-6

		24	15
3	1		3
		2	4
30		6	5

12. Use 1-6

		3	10
4	1		4
		2	6
15	3	5	

Page 73

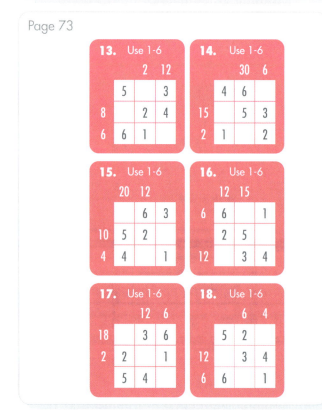

13. Use 1-6

		2	12
	5		3
8		2	4
6	6	1	

14. Use 1-6

		30	6
	4	6	
15		5	3
2	1		2

15. Use 1-6

		20	12
		6	3
10	5	2	
4	4		1

16. Use 1-6

		12	15
6	6		1
	2	5	
12		3	4

17. Use 1-6

		12	6
18		3	6
2	2		1
	5	4	

18. Use 1-6

		6	4
	5	2	
12		3	4
6	6		1

Page 74

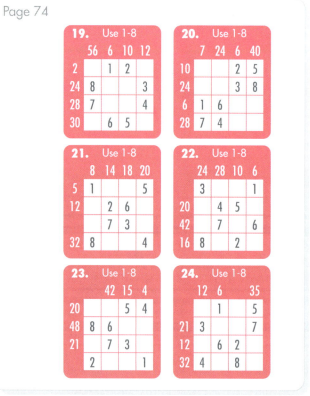

19. Use 1-8

	56	6	10	12
2		1	2	
24	8			3
28	7			4
30		6	5	

20. Use 1-8

	7	24	6	40
10			2	5
24			3	8
6	1	6		
28	7	4		

21. Use 1-8

	8	14	18	20
5	1			5
12		2	6	
		7	3	
32	8			4

22. Use 1-8

	24	28	10	6
	3			1
20		4	5	
42		7		6
16	8		2	

23. Use 1-8

	42	15	4
20		5	4
48	8	6	
21		7	3
2			1

24. Use 1-8

	12	6		35
		1		5
21	3			7
12		6	2	
32	4		8	

Page 75

25. Use 1-8

	2	56	12	
35	5		7	
18	6			3
		2	8	
4		1	4	

26. Use 1-8

	24	6	20	
40		8		5
24			6	4
6	2	3		
	7		1	

27. Use 1-8

	20	6	21	
24	4	6		
6			3	2
8		1		8
	5		7	

28. Use 1-8

	24	6	14	
6		3		2
24	4		6	
		8		7
5	5		1	

29. Use 1-8

	24	40	6	
6	6			1
8	4		2	
		5		7
24	8	3		

30. Use 1-8

	24	8	6	
24			4	6
8		8		1
14	7		2	
	5	3		

Page 76

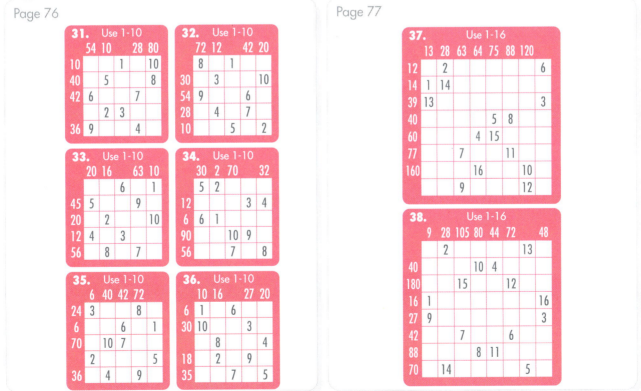

31. Use 1-10

	54	10		28	80
10			1		10
40		5			8
42	6			7	
			2	3	
36	9			4	

32. Use 1-10

	72	12		42	20
	8		1		
30		3			10
54	9			6	
28		4		7	
10			5		2

33. Use 1-10

	20	16		63	10
			6		1
45	5			9	
20		2			10
12	4				
56		8		7	

34. Use 1-10

	30	2	70		32
	5	2			
12				3	4
6	6	1			
90			10	9	
56			7		8

35. Use 1-10

	6	40	42	72	
24	3			8	
6			6		1
70		10	7		
	2				5
36		4		9	

36. Use 1-10

	10	16		27	20
6	1		6		
30	10			3	
			8		4
18		2		9	
35			7		5

Page 77

37. Use 1-16

	13	28	63	64	75	88	120
12		2					6
14	1	14					
39	13						3
40				5	8		
60			4	15			
77		7			11		
160			16			10	
		9				12	

38. Use 1-16

	9	28	105	80	44	72		48
		2				13		
40			10	4				
180		15			12			
16	1							16
27	9						3	
42			7		6			
88			8	11				
70	14					5		

PRODUCT SQUARES SOLUTIONS

Page 83

1.

2	24	3
3	4	5
21	7	35

2.

7	35	5
5	1	20
25	5	4

3.

4	6	18
16	2	3
2	28	7

4.

2	3	4
12	15	12
6	5	3

5.

10	2	12
5	60	6
6	48	8

6.

6	3	2
6	12	1
1	4	4

7.

16	8	8
2	4	1
10	5	5

8.

30	6	24
5	2	4
4	16	2

Page 84

9.

1	12	4
15	3	24
5	30	2

10.

20	5	25
4	300	5
12	3	15

11.

32	4	5
8	2	20
4	16	2

12.

5	25	1
6	5	30
42	7	6

13.

28	7	5	5
4	3	15	1
7	21	1	3

14.

9	36	4	20
27	1	3	5
3	6	2	10

15.

1	6	2	8
9	3	24	4
3	9	1	4

16.

4	36	9	1
9	36	4	20
8	8	1	5

Page 85

17.

3	36	2	10
2	6	3	5
14	7	42	2

18.

6	5	60	3
54	9	4	24
1	45	5	2

19.

18	2	4	24
9	3	360	6
36	4	5	30

20.

12	2	6	12
6	48	4	2
3	27	9	18

21.

9	81	64	8
6	9	8	7
36	6	7	49

22.

25	5	2	4
5	75	32	2
15	3	8	16

23.

3	9	54	6
9	3	1	18
1	5	15	3

24.

32	8	48	2
4	2	3	30
8	16	15	5

Page 86

25.

3	75	5	2
1	5	7	70
15	3	4	5
5	7	84	3

26.

7	21	3	12
42	1	24	4
6	3	2	40
1	12	4	5

27.

5	35	40	8
4	7	5	80
60	5	1	2
3	2	10	5

28.

25	5	7	14
5	100	4	2
6	1	5	10
24	4	20	1

29.

8	1	28	7
56	7	4	1
1	2	7	21
7	14	1	3

30.

6	24	2	4
12	2	4	16
24	8	6	12
3	4	48	2

31.

2	1	5	7	42
2	5	75	3	6
18	3	1	5	30
3	36	4	20	1

32.

5	5	25	1	3
1	25	5	45	3
9	1	2	3	36
9	3	12	2	4

33.

16	4	8	1	9
4	1	2	72	9
6	36	3	4	8
12	2	18	3	24

34.

7	1	14	2	5
1	49	7	5	75
28	7	2	30	3
4	2	4	1	6

35.

2	1	3	12	4
8	4	7	70	2
1	8	2	5	30
8	8	1	2	3

36.

2	12	12	6	4
1	6	2	12	8
6	24	4	1	2
6	1	4	8	8

37.

3	5	7	7	1
3	75	5	1	3
1	3	9	27	21
5	15	1	3	7

38.

4	3	15	5	5
64	8	5	1	2
2	1	3	8	16
8	8	9	3	1

39.

1	3	12	4	2
28	4	1	2	12
7	5	25	1	3
7	1	5	3	9

40.

1	10	2	12	3
3	5	1	2	4
6	1	5	4	16
2	3	75	5	1

41.

1	20	4	12	3
10	5	2	1	24
2	1	8	4	8
8	8	1	8	2

42.

2	12	6	1	4
7	1	2	12	3
1	21	3	2	7
3	7	1	4	2

43.

5	35	1	7	35
70	7	2	70	5
2	84	6	1	20
18	1	3	48	4
9	5	8	4	7

44.

3	27	9	18	2
5	15	3	6	10
7	1	4	2	5
7	8	8	48	3
1	6	6	24	4

45.

30	6	5	70	7
5	3	60	2	4
40	8	2	7	56
1	5	80	8	2
4	20	1	5	10

46.

54	6	12	1	5
9	3	2	7	5
54	1	12	2	40
6	8	3	9	4
24	4	60	5	20

47.

6	1	3	6	24
6	3	9	1	4
4	24	1	20	5
3	2	56	4	6
18	6	7	2	12

48.

4	1	9	36	4
4	84	3	1	32
5	7	2	6	8
30	3	1	60	2
2	24	4	5	10

ARRANGING SQUARES SOLUTIONS

Page 95

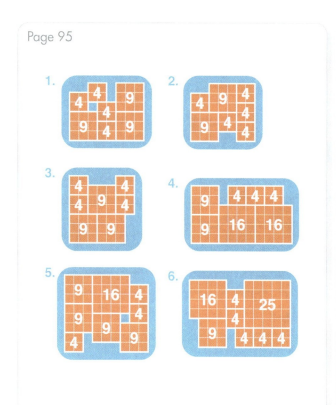

1.
2.
3.
4.
5.
6.

Page 96

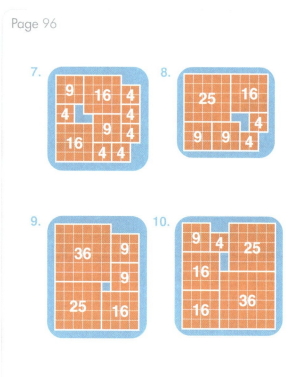

7.
8.
9.
10.

Page 97

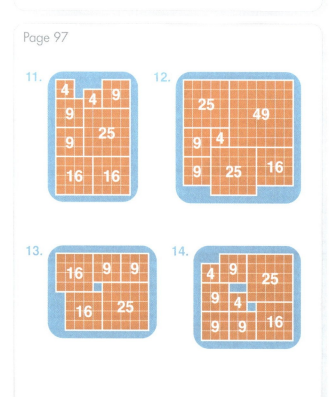

11.
12.
13.
14.

Page 98

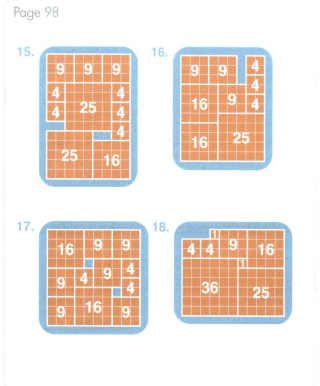

15.
16.
17.
18.

19.

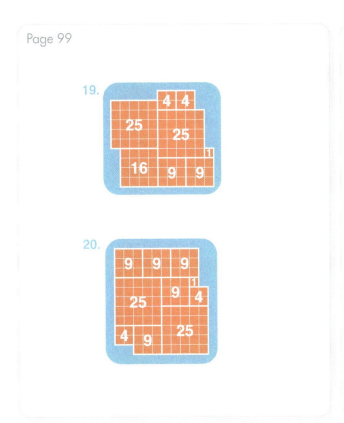

20.

21.

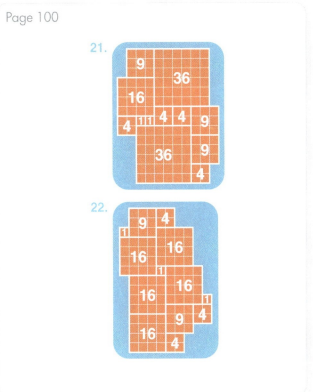

22.

23.

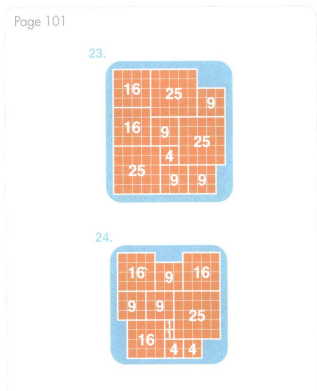

24.

25.

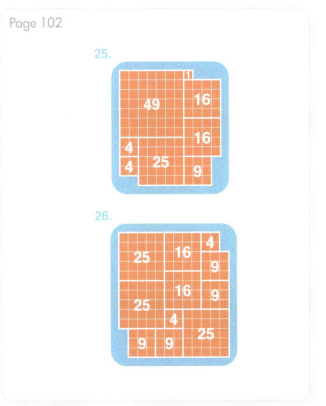

26.

Page 103

27.

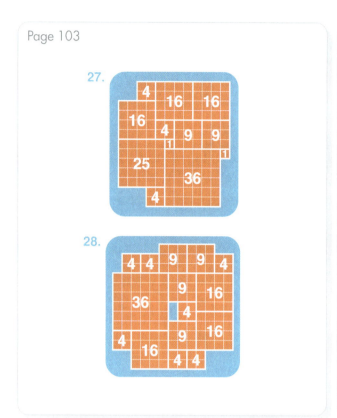

28.

Page 104

29.

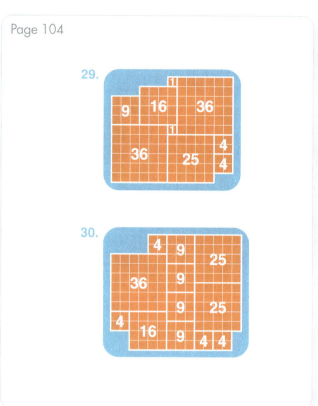

30.

Page 105

31.

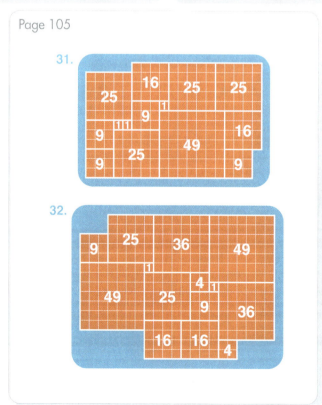

32.

Beast Academy Puzzles 3 - Solutions

CIRCLE SUMS SOLUTIONS

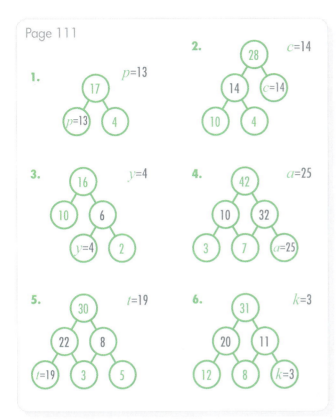

Page 111

1. *p*=13
17
p=13 4

2. *c*=14
28
14 *c*=14
10 4

3. *y*=4
16
10 6
y=4 2

4. *a*=25
42
10 32
3 7 *a*=25

5. *t*=19
30
22 8
t=19 3 5

6. *k*=3
31
20 11
12 8 *k*=3

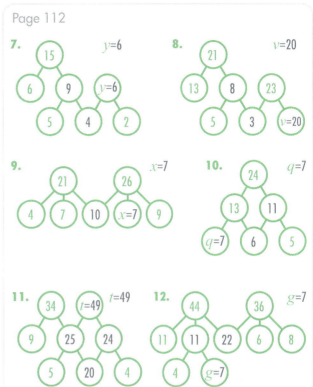

Page 112

7. *y*=6
15
6 9 *y*=6
5 4 2

8. *v*=20
21
13 8 23
5 3 *v*=20

9. *x*=7
21 26
4 7 10 *x*=7 9

10. *q*=7
24
13 11
q=7 6 5

11. *t*=49
34 *t*=49
9 25 24
5 20 4

12. *g*=7
44 36
11 11 22 6 8
4 *g*=7

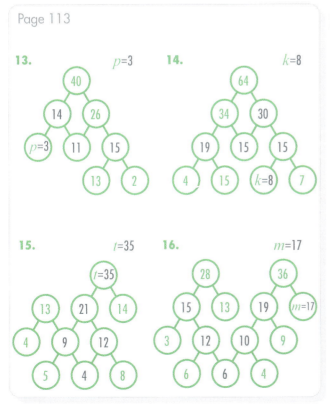

Page 113

13. *p*=3
40
14 26
p=3 11 15
13 2

14. *k*=8
64
34 30
19 15 15
4 15 *k*=8 7

15. *t*=35
t=35
13 21 14
4 9 12
5 4 8

16. *m*=17
28 36
15 13 19 *m*=17
3 12 10 9
6 6 4

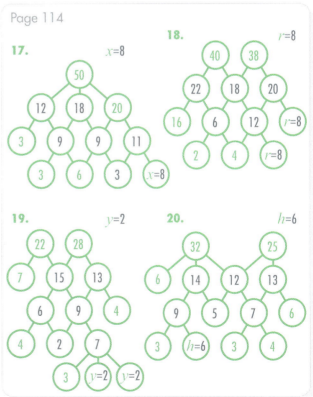

Page 114

17. *x*=8
50
12 18 20
3 9 9 11
3 6 3 *x*=8

18. *r*=8
40 38
22 18 20
16 6 12 *r*=8
2 4 *r*=8

19. *y*=2
22 28
7 15 13
6 9 4
4 2 7
3 *y*=2 *y*=2

20. *h*=6
32 25
6 14 12 13
9 5 7 6
3 *h*=6 3 4

Beast Academy Puzzles 3 - Solutions

Page 115

21.
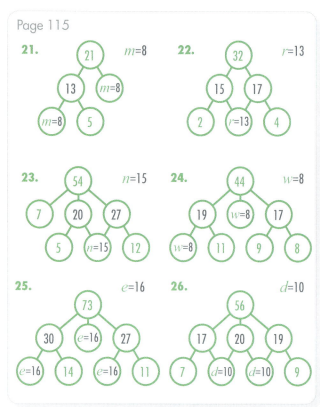

22.

23. $n=15$

24. $w=8$

25. $e=16$

26. $d=10$

Page 116

27. $x=2$, $y=7$

28. $a=1$, $b=6$

29. $j=7$, $k=4$

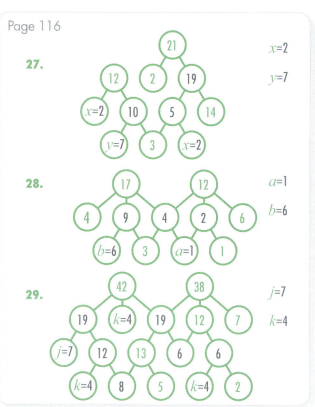

Page 117

30. $g=5$, $h=2$

31. $r=2$, $s=3$

32. $m=4$, $n=9$

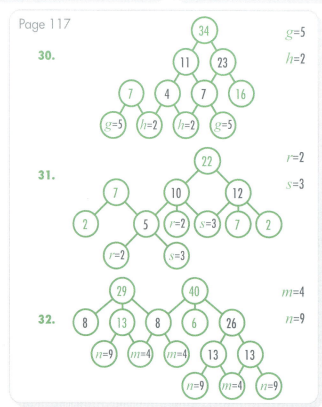

Page 118

33. a=3

34. j=6

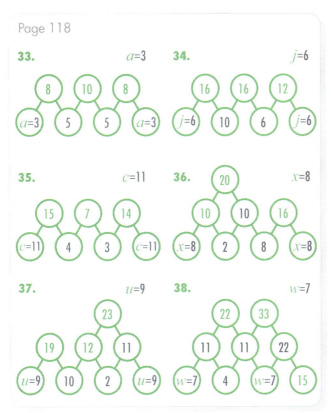

35. c=11

36. x=8

37. u=9

38. w=7

Page 119

39. h=6

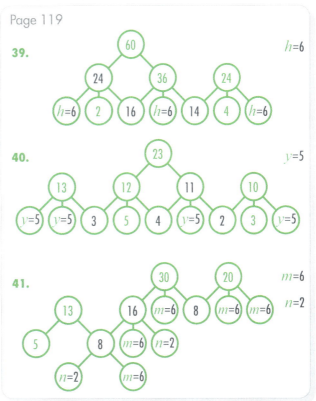

40. y=5

41. m=6
                           n=2

FRACTION LINK SOLUTIONS

Page 123

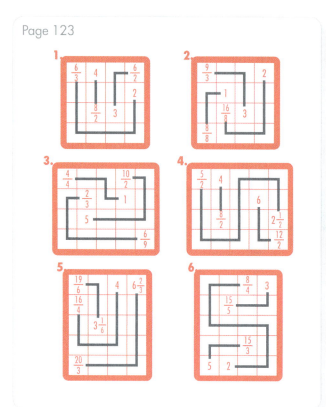

Page 124

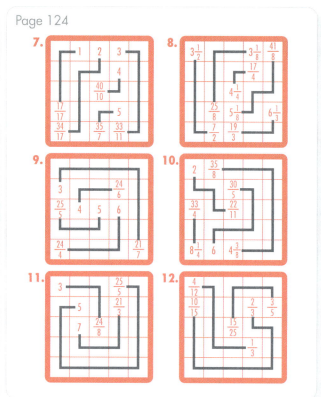

Page 125

Page 126

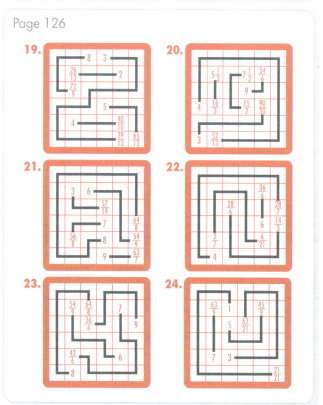

Page 127

25.

26.

27.

28.

29.

30.

Page 128

31.

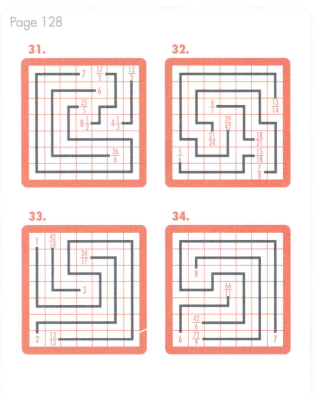

32.

33.

34.

Page 129

35.

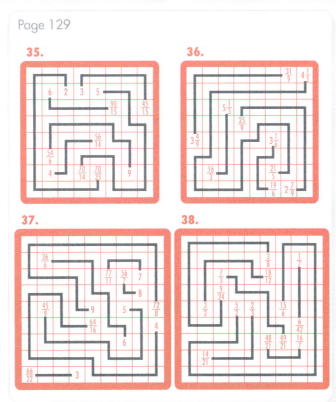

36.

37.

38.

ABSTRACT ART SOLUTIONS

Page 135

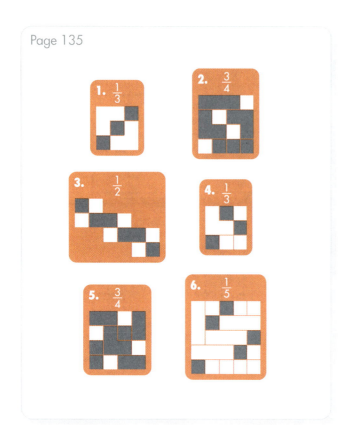

Page 136

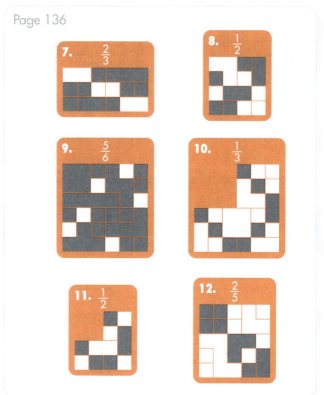

Page 137

Page 138

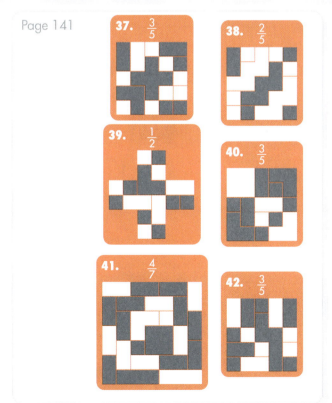

Page 142

Page 143

Beast Academy Puzzles 3 - Solutions

SHIKAKU SOLUTIONS

Page 149

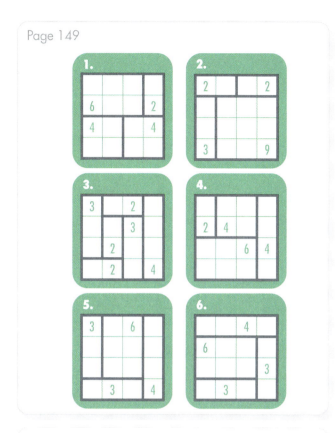

Page 150

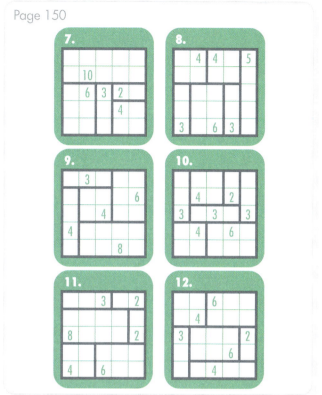

Page 151

Page 152

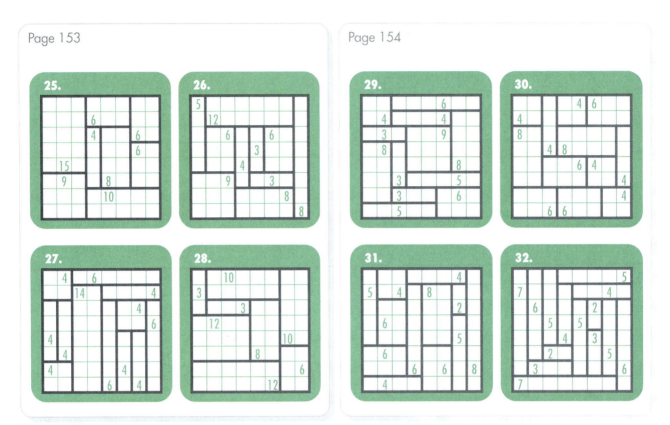

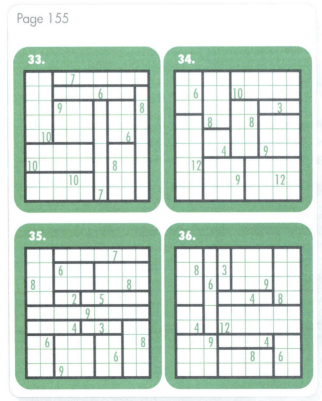

Page 156

37.

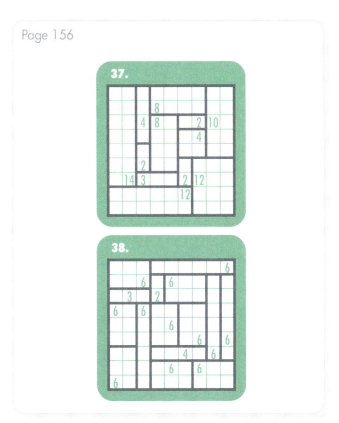

38.

Page 157

39.

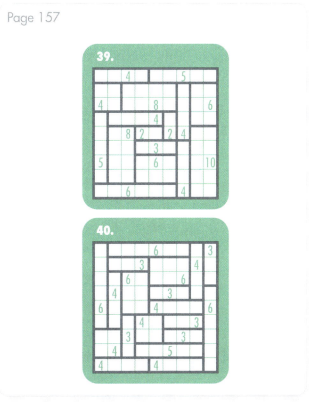

40.

WANT MORE BEAST ACADEMY?

Try our complete math curriculum!

- **Books**

  The Beast Academy book series is a comprehensive, rigorous, and engaging math curriculum for ages 8-13. This book is part of the level 3 series.

- **Online**

  Beast Academy Online is a complete online math program for ages 8-13 with more than 800 lessons, 700 videos, 15,000 problems and puzzles (including a dedicated Puzzle Lab), plus digital versions of the Beast Academy Guide books.

Learn more at BeastAcademy.com.